EASY PIANO

TOP50 Christmas Hits

Arranged by Dan Coates

Alfred Music
P.O. Box 10003
Van Nuys, CA 91410-0003
alfred.com

ISBN-10: 0-7390-6213-1
ISBN-13: 978-0-7390-6213-5

TABLE OF CONTENTS

ALL I WANT FOR CHRISTMAS
IS MY TWO FRONT TEETH

Words and Music by Don Gardner
Arranged by Dan Coates

ANGELS WE HAVE HEARD ON HIGH

Traditional Carol
Arranged by Dan Coates

Chorus:

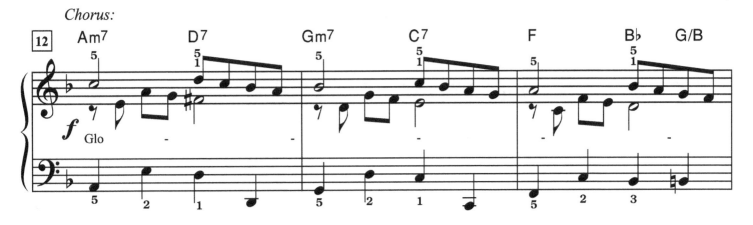

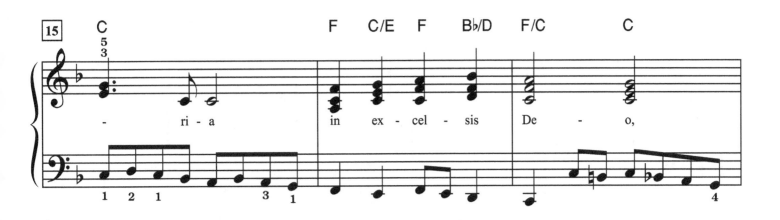

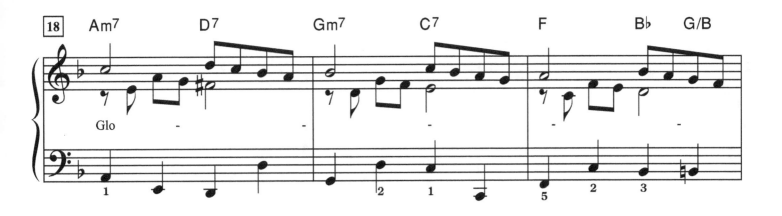

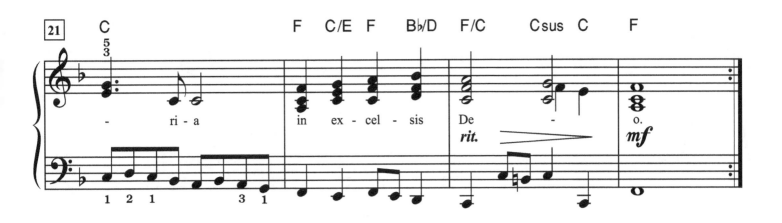

THE ANNUAL ANIMAL CHRISTMAS BALL

Words and Music by
George David Weiss
Arranged by Dan Coates

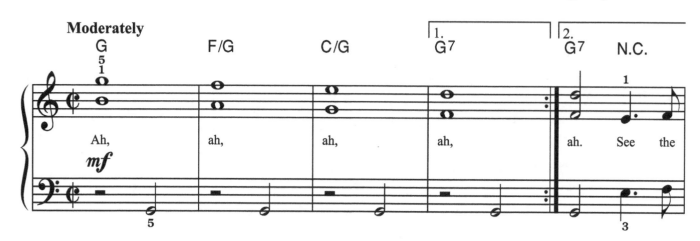

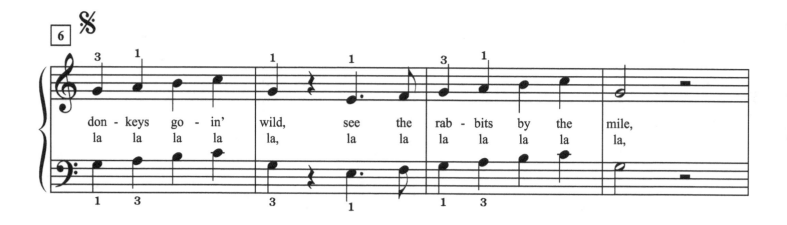

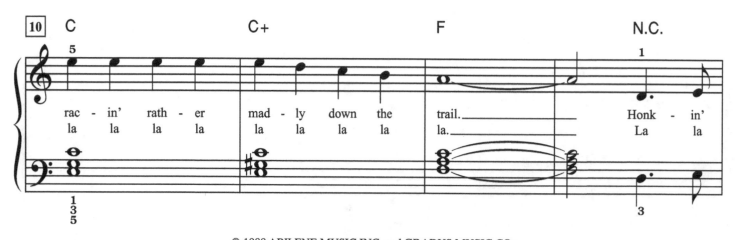

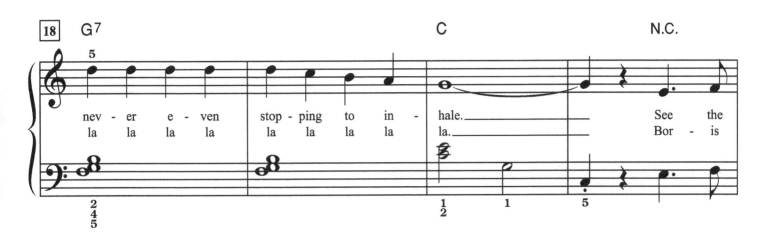

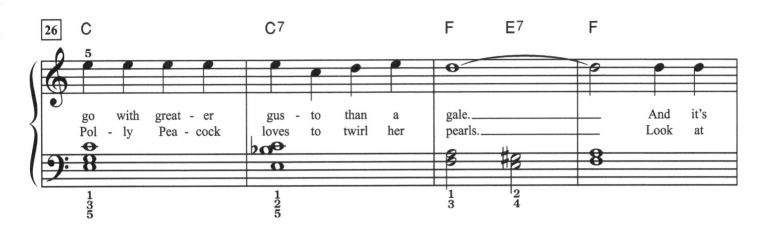

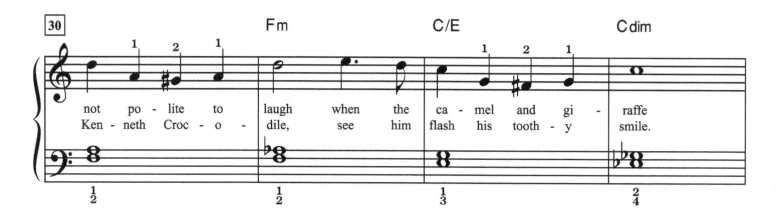

not po - lite to laugh when the ca - mel and gi - raffe
Ken - neth Croc - o - dile, see him flash his tooth - y smile.

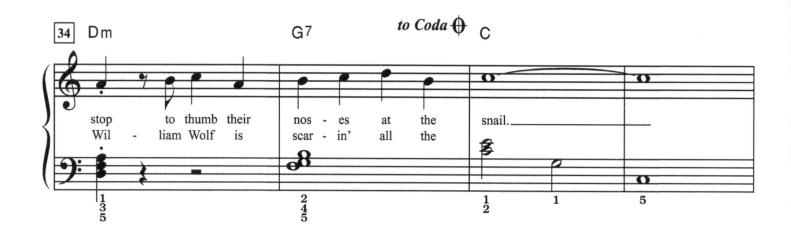

stop to thumb their nos - es at the snail._____
Wil - liam Wolf is scar - in' all the

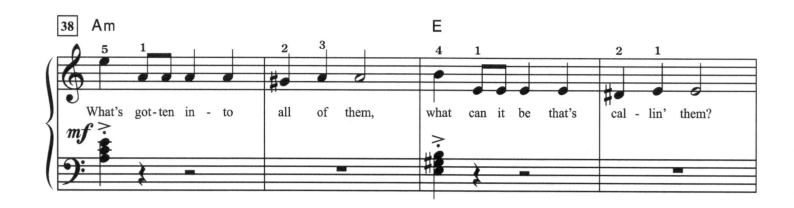

What's got-ten in - to all of them, what can it be that's cal - lin' them?

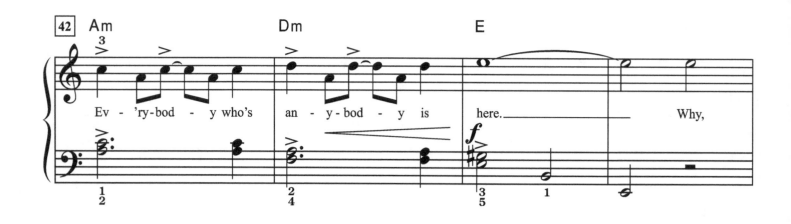

Ev - 'ry-bod - y who's an - y-bod - y is here._____ Why,

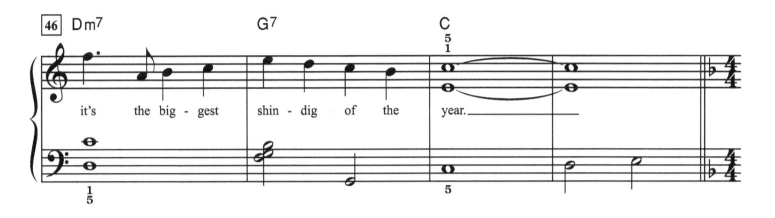

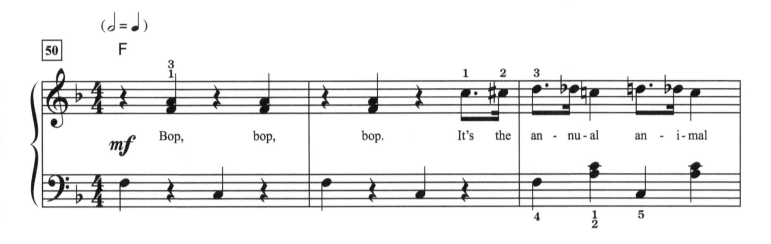

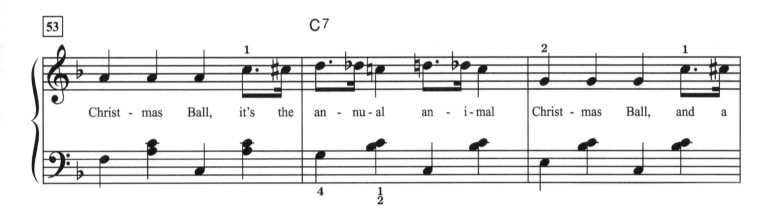

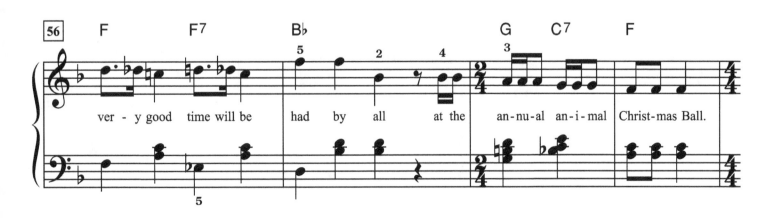

60

Nel - lie El - e-phant grace-ful-ly taps her toe. Tes - sie

63 C7   F   F7

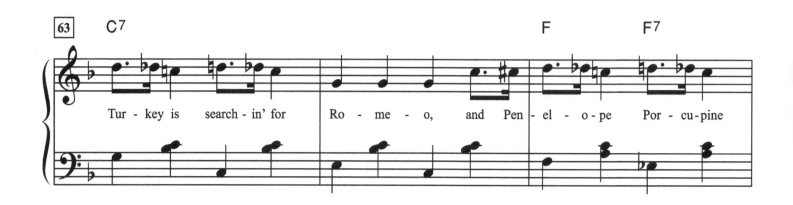

Tur - key is search - in' for Ro - me - o, and Pen - el - o - pe Por - cu-pine

66 B♭   G   C7   (♩=♩)   *D.S. al Coda*

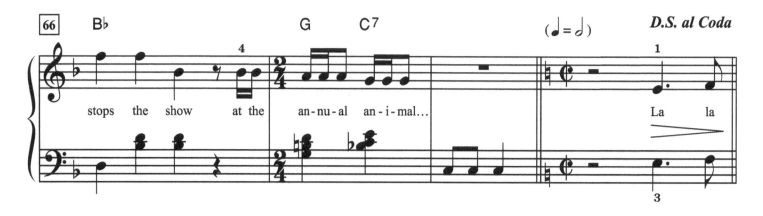

stops the show at the an-nu-al an-i-mal...   La la

Coda
(♩=♩)
C   F

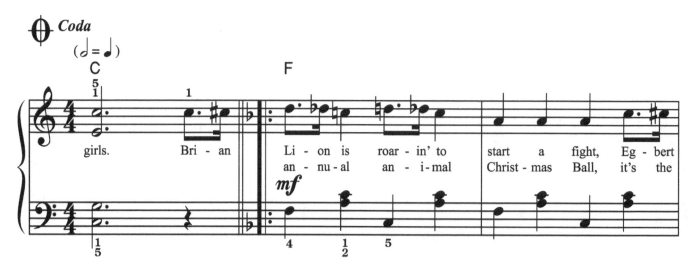

girls. Bri - an Li - on is roar - in' to start a fight, Eg - bert
                       an - nu - al an - i - mal Christ - mas Ball, it's the

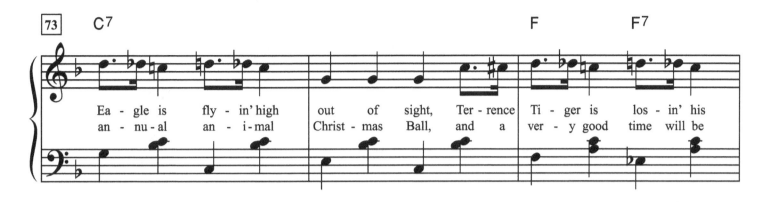

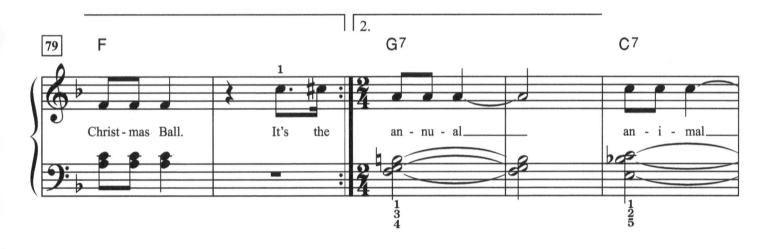

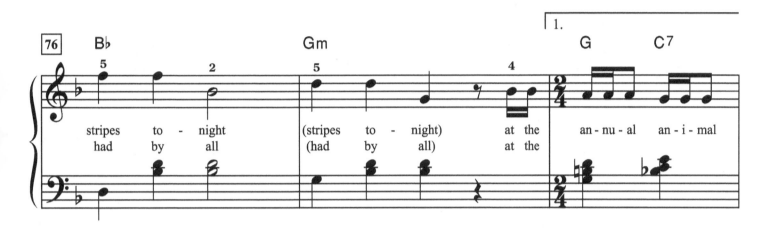

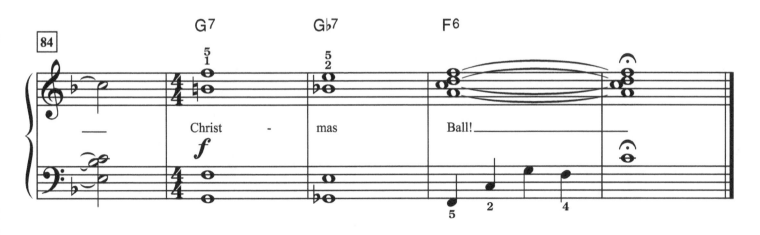

AWAY IN A MANGER

Words by Anonymous
Music by James R. Murray
Arranged by Dan Coates

BELIEVE

Words and Music by
Alan Silvestri and Glenn Ballard
Arranged by Dan Coates

Moderately slow

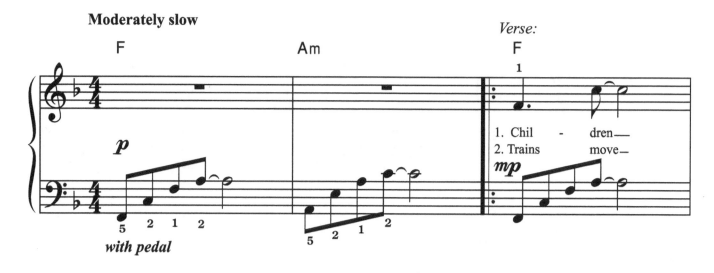

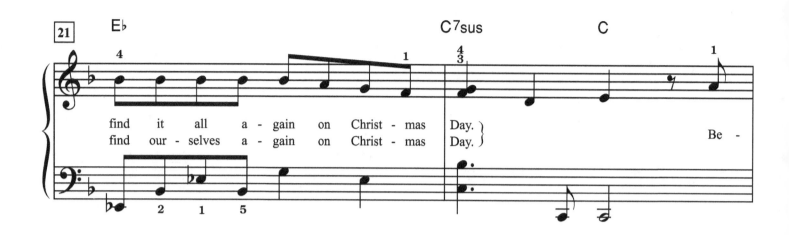

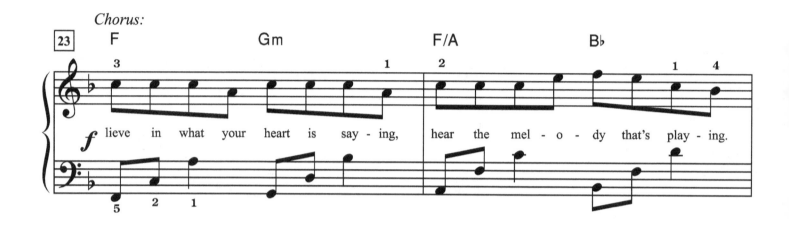

Chorus:

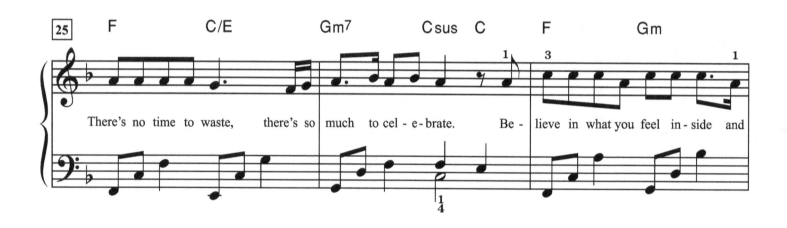

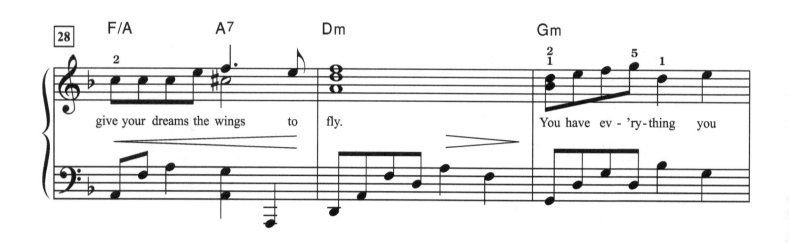

THE COVENTRY CAROL

Traditional English Carol
Arranged by Dan Coates

Verse 2:
O sisters, too, how may we do,
For to preserve this day
This poor youngling for whom we sing
By, by, lully, lullay.

Verse 3:
Herod the king, in his raging,
Charged he hath this day
His men of might, in his own sight,
All children young to slay.

Verse 4:
Then woe is me, poor Child, for Thee!
And ever morn and day,
For Thy parting nor say nor sing,
By, by, lully, lullay.

DECK THE HALLS

Traditional Carol
Arranged by Dan Coates

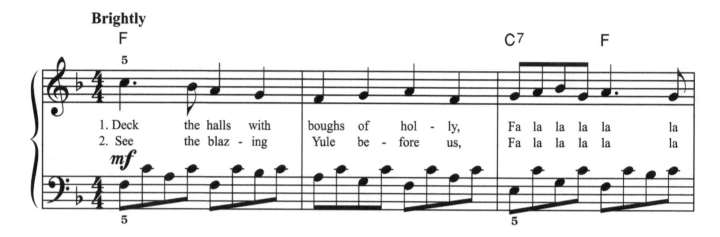

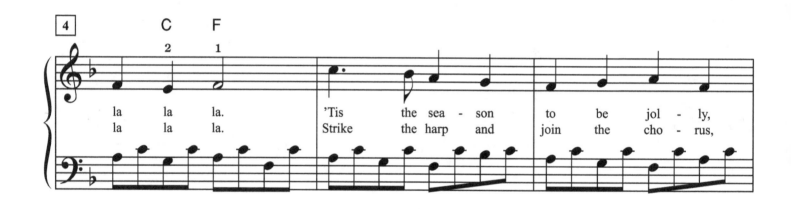

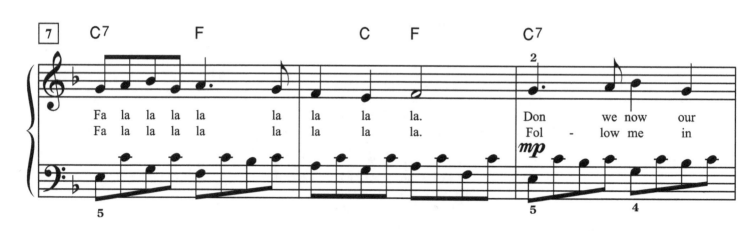

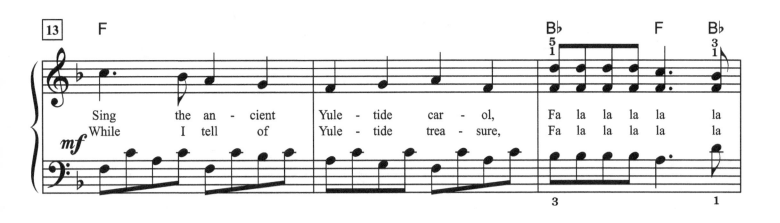

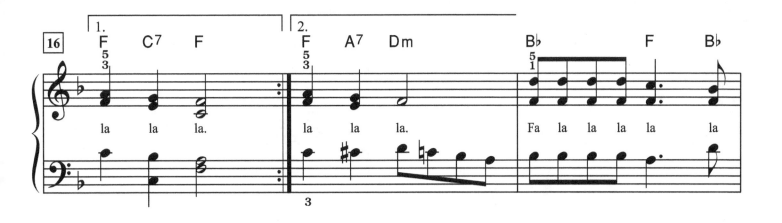

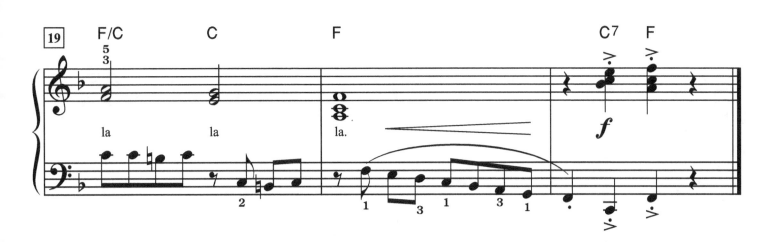

THE CHRISTMAS WALTZ

Words by Sammy Cahn
Music by Jule Styne
Arranged by Dan Coates

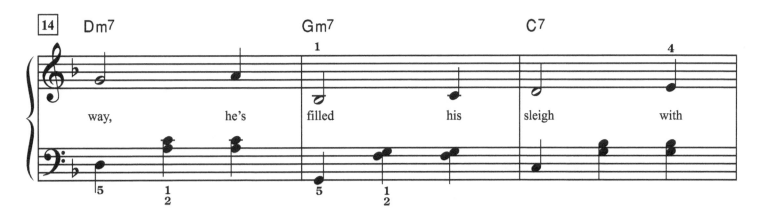

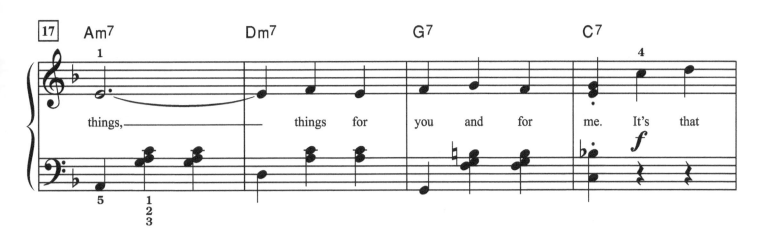

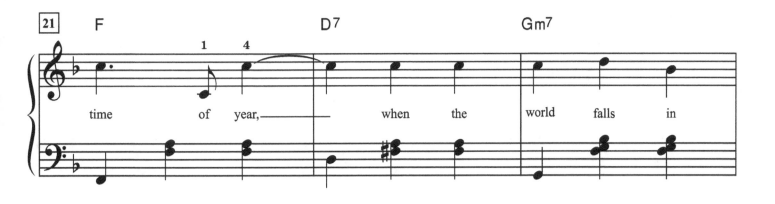

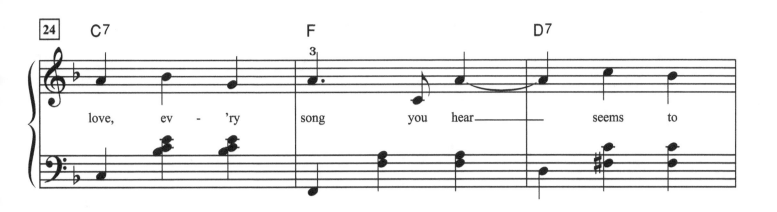

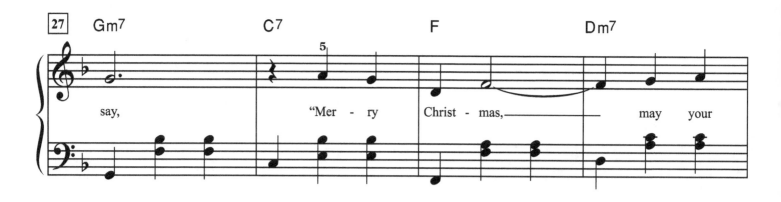

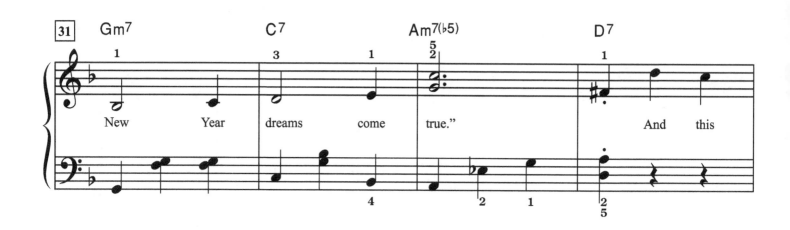

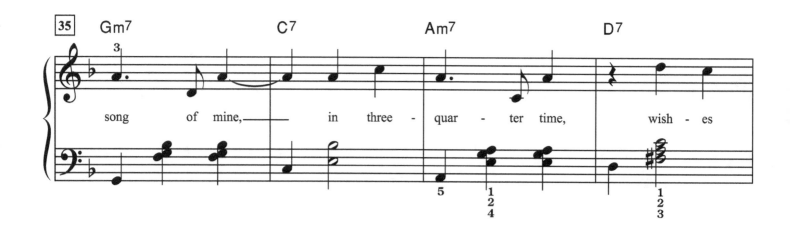

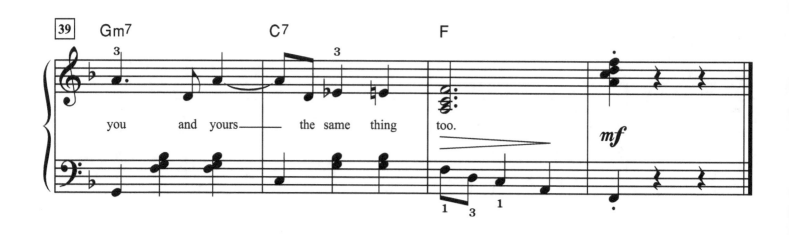

FROSTY THE SNOWMAN

Words and Music by
Steve Nelson and Jack Rollins
Arranged by Dan Coates

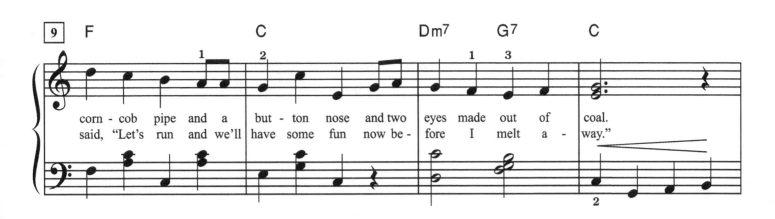

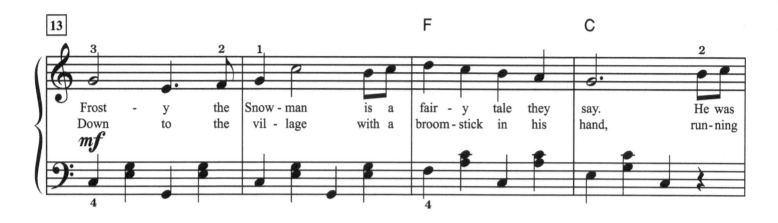

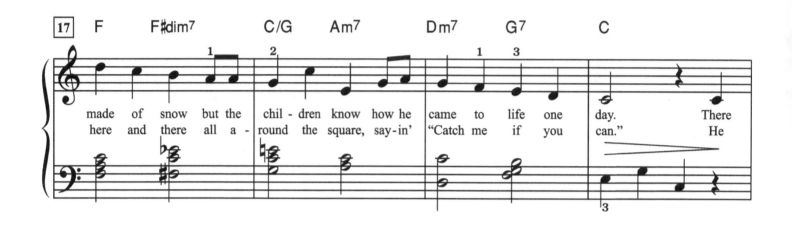

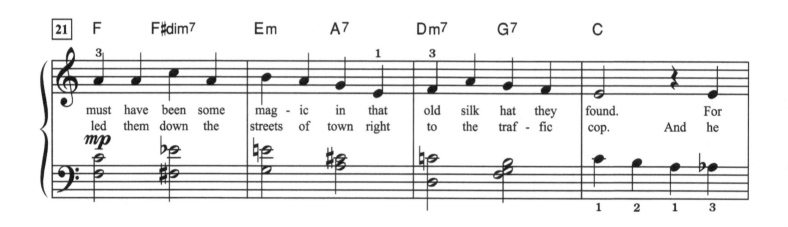

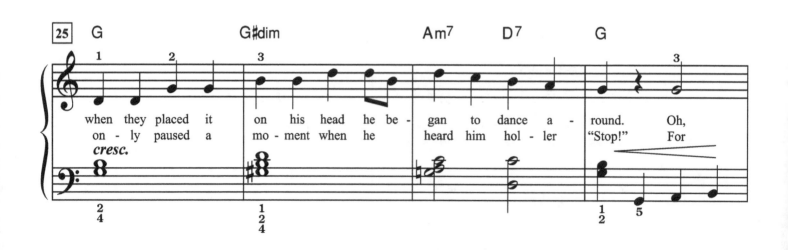

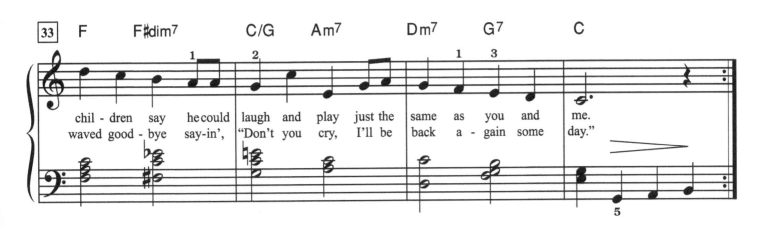

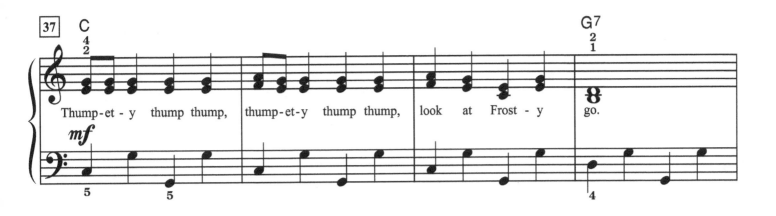

THE FIRST NOEL

Traditional Carol
Arranged by Dan Coates

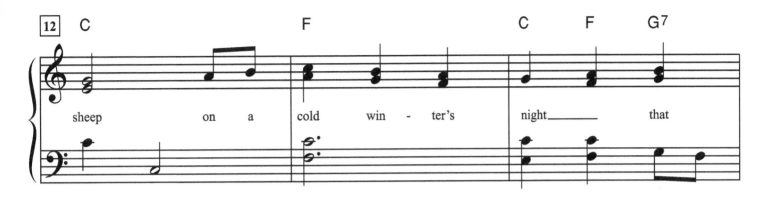

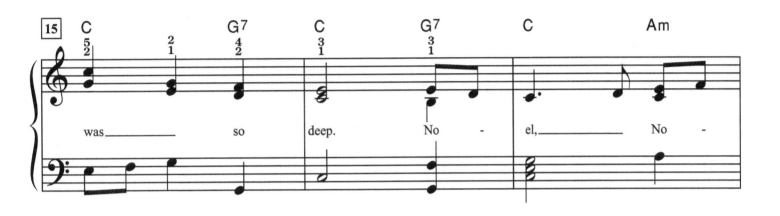

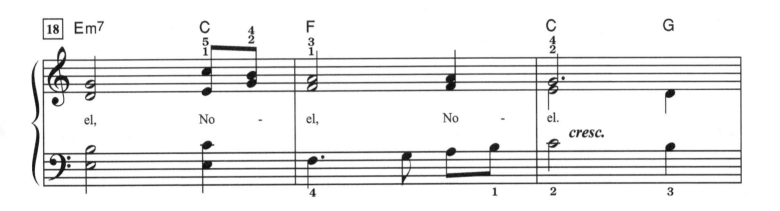

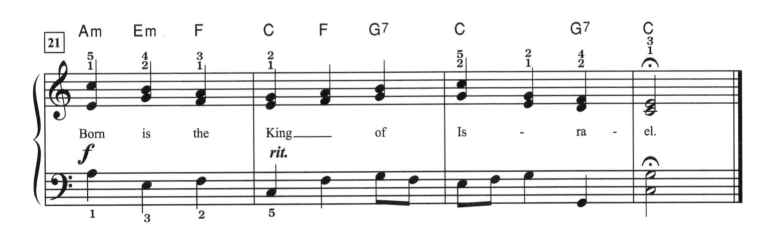

THE FRUITCAKE THAT ATE NEW JERSEY

Words and Music by Lauren Mayer
Arranged by Dan Coates

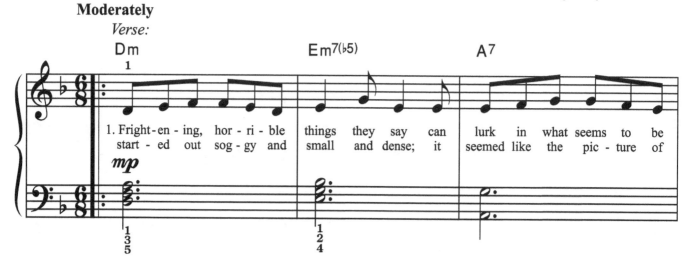

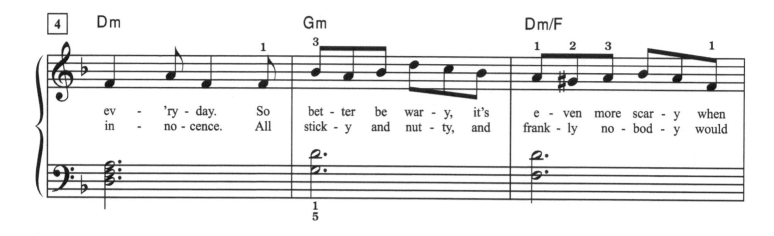

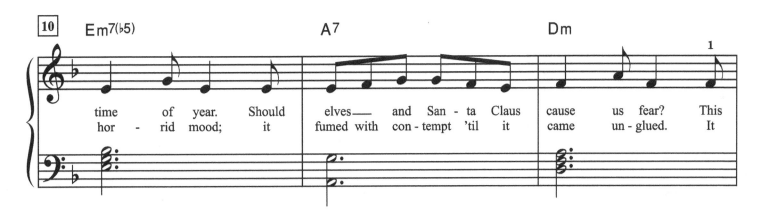

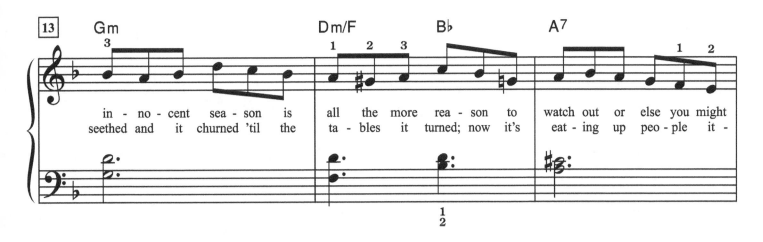

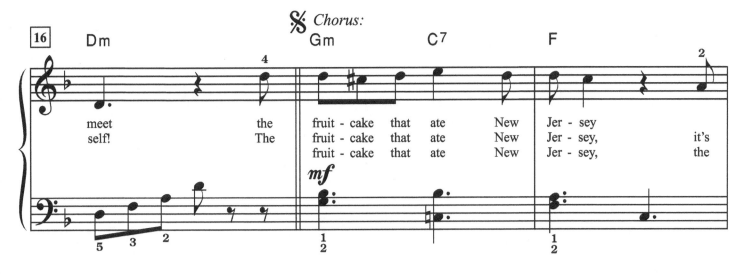

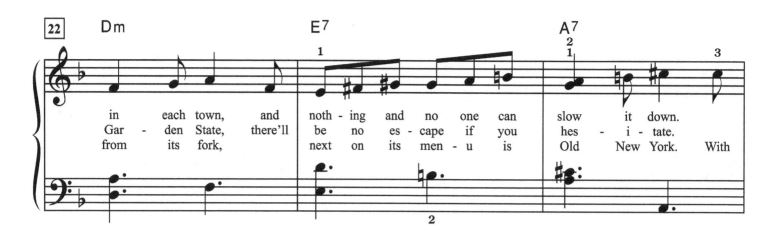

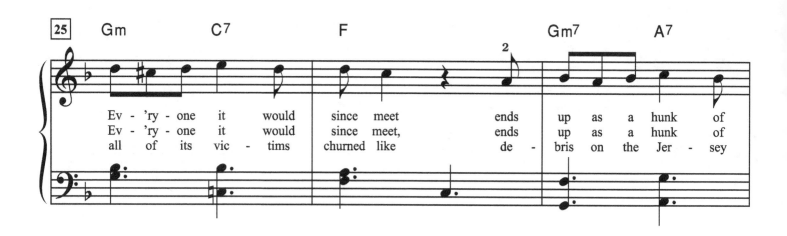

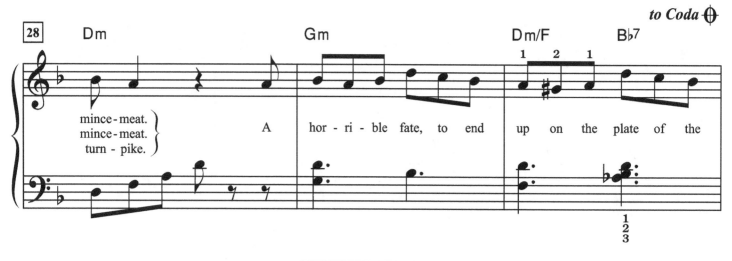

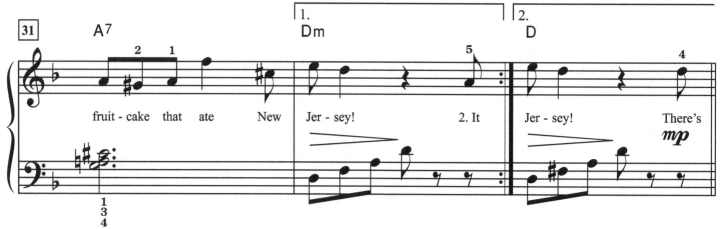

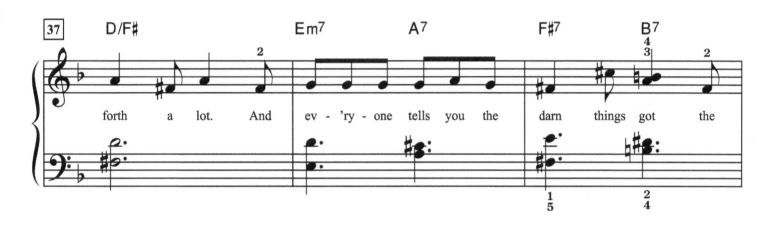

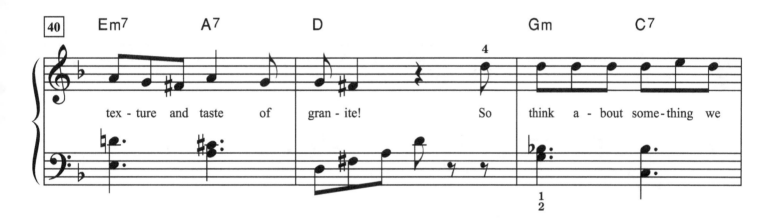

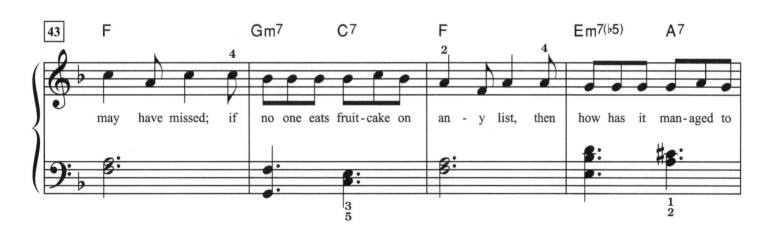

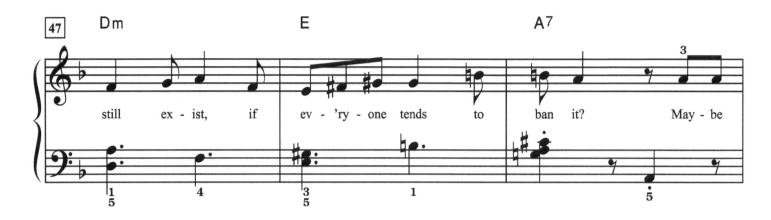

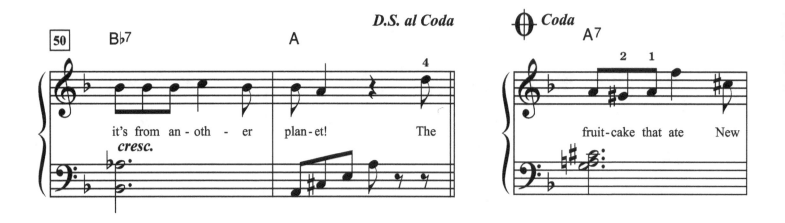

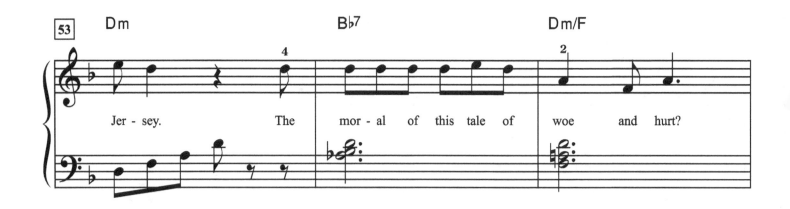

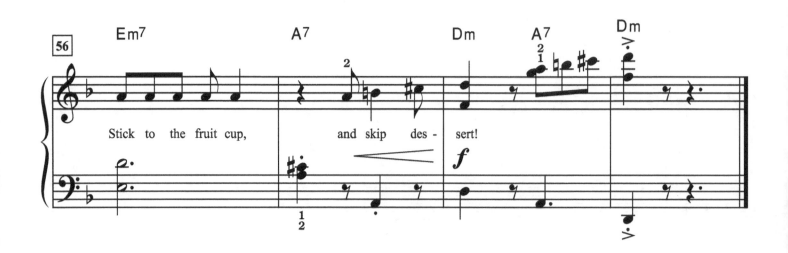

GRANDMA GOT RUN OVER BY A REINDEER

Words and Music by Randy Brooks
Arranged by Dan Coates

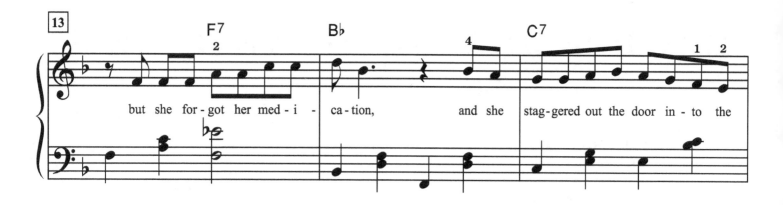

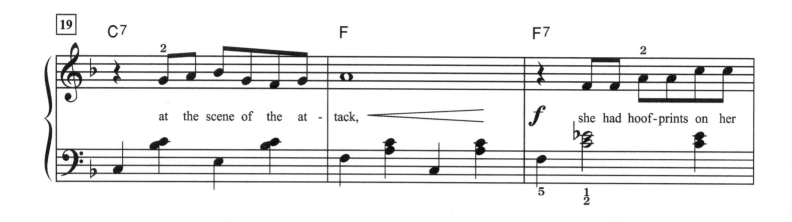

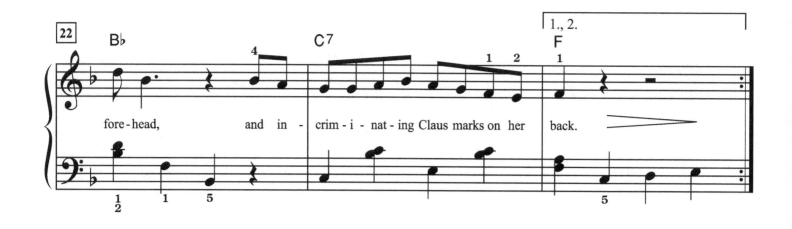

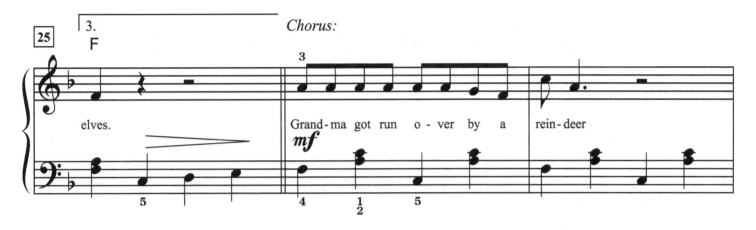

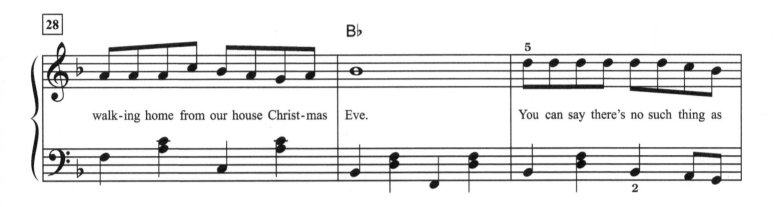

Verse 2:
Now we're all so proud of Grandpa,
He's been taking this so well.
See him in there watching football,
Drinking beer and playing cards with Cousin Mel.
It's not Christmas without Grandma.
All the family's dressed in black,
And we just can't help but wonder:
Should we open up her gifts or send them back?
(To Chorus:)

Verse 3:
Now the goose is on the table,
And the pudding made of fig,
And the blue and silver candles,
That would just have matched the hair in Grandma's wig.
I've warned all my friends and neighbors,
Better watch out for yourselves.
They should never give a license
To a man who drives a sleigh and plays with elves.
(To Chorus:)

GOD REST YE MERRY, GENTLEMEN

Traditional Carol
Arranged by Dan Coates

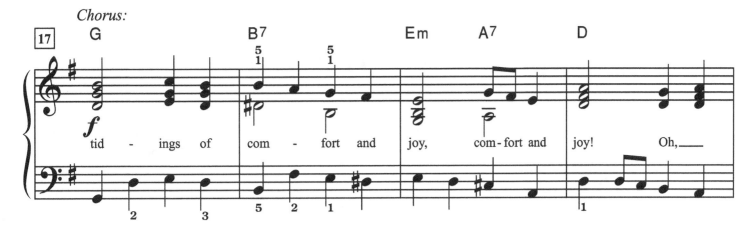

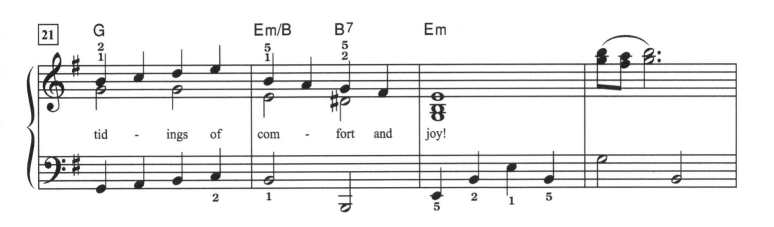

Verse 2:
In Bethlehem, in Israel, this blessed babe was born,
And laid within a manger upon this blessed morn;
The which His mother Mary did nothing take in scorn.
(To Chorus:)

Verse 3:
From God our Heavenly Father, a blessed angel came,
And unto certain shepherds brought tidings of the same;
How that in Bethlehem was born the Son of God by name.
(To Chorus:)

GOOD KING WENCESLAS

Traditional Carol
Arranged by Dan Coates

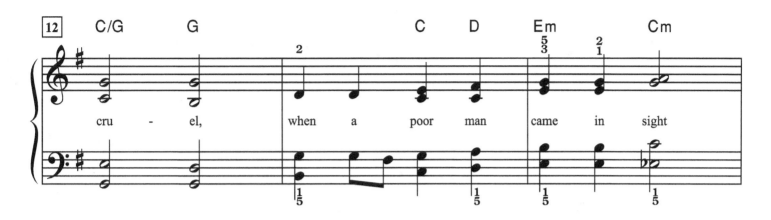

cru - el, when a poor man came in sight

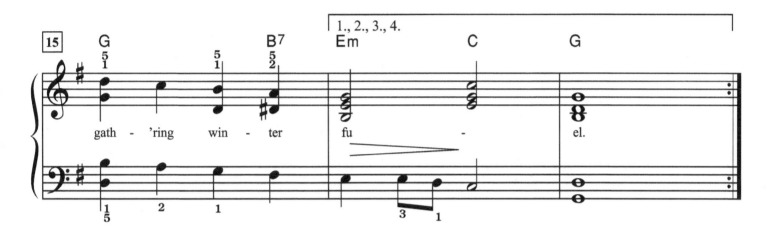

gath - 'ring win - ter fu - el.

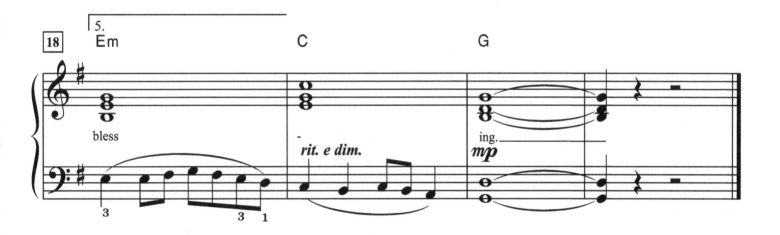

bless - ing.

rit. e dim.

mp

Verse 2:
"Hither, page, and stand by me, if thou know'st it, telling,
Yonder peasant, who is he? Where and what his dwelling?"
"Sire, he lives a good league hence, underneath the mountain,
Right against the forest fence, by Saint Agnes' Fountain."

Verse 3:
"Bring me flesh and bring me wine, bring me pine logs hither.
Thou and I will see him dine when we bear him thither."
Page and monarch forth they went, forth they went together,
Through the rude wind's wild lament and the bitter weather.

Verse 4:
"Sire, the night is darker now, and the wind blows stronger.
Fails my heart, I know not how, I can go no longer."
"Mark my footsteps, my good page, tread thou in them boldy.
Thou shalt find the winter's rage freeze thy blood less coldly."

Verse 5:
In his master's steps he trod, where the snow lay dinted.
Heat was in the very sod which the Saint had printed.
Therefore, Christian men, be sure, wealth or rank possessing;
Ye who now will bless the poor shall yourselves find blessing.

HARK! THE HERALD ANGELS SING

Traditional Carol
Arranged by Dan Coates

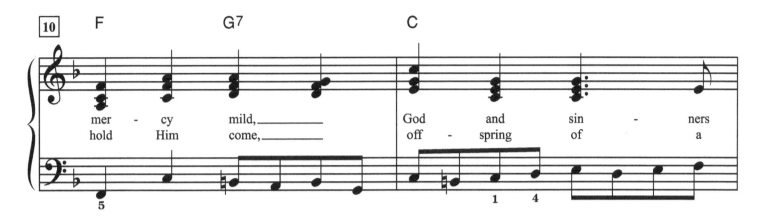

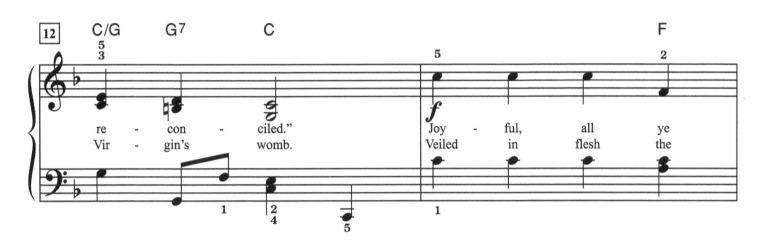

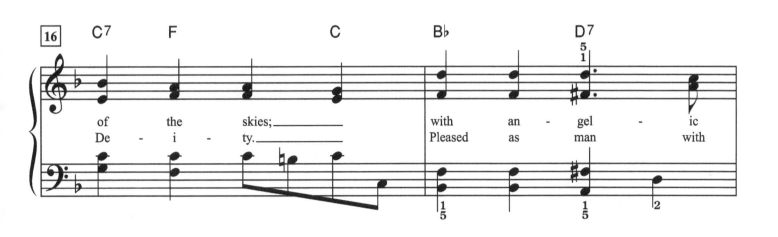

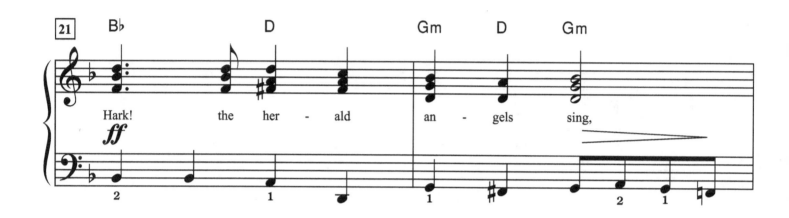

HAVE YOURSELF A
MERRY LITTLE CHRISTMAS

Words and Music by
Hugh Martin and Ralph Blane
Arranged by Dan Coates

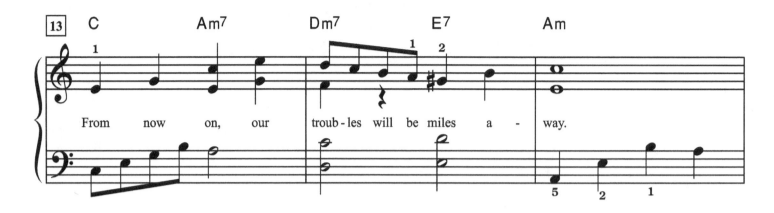

13 From now on, our troub-les will be miles a - way.

16 Here we are as in old-en days, hap-py

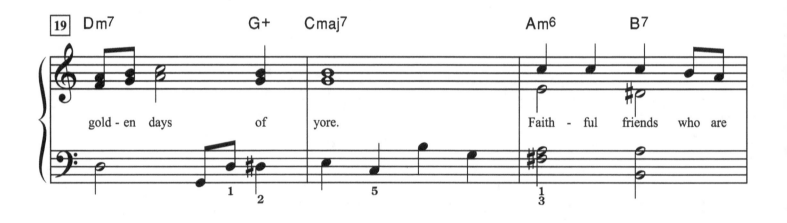

19 gold-en days of yore. Faith-ful friends who are

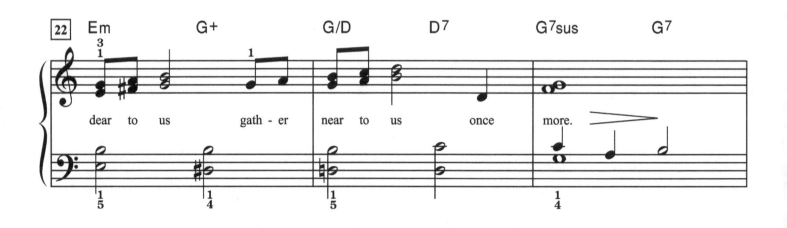

22 dear to us gath-er near to us once more.

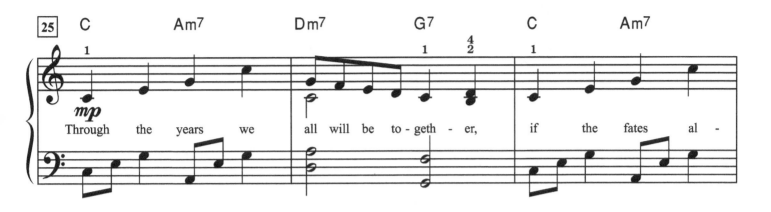

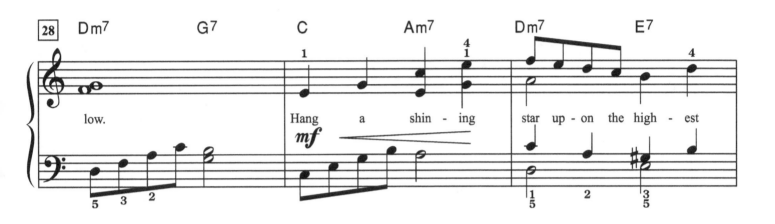

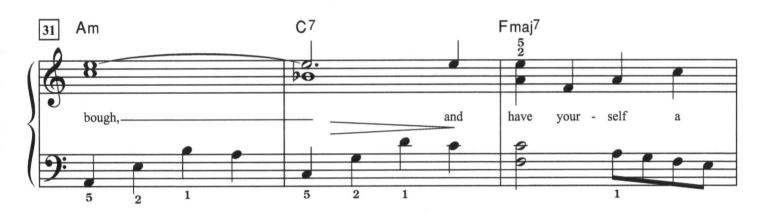

(THERE'S NO PLACE LIKE) HOME FOR THE HOLIDAYS

Words by Al Stillman
Music by Robert Allen
Arranged by Dan Coates

51

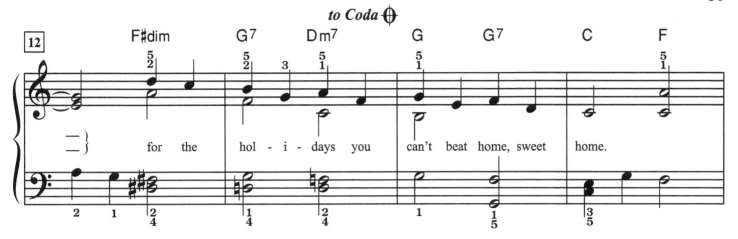

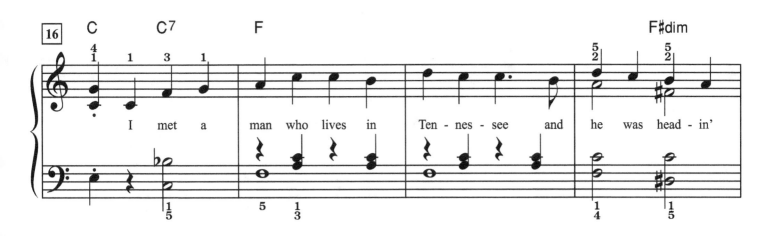

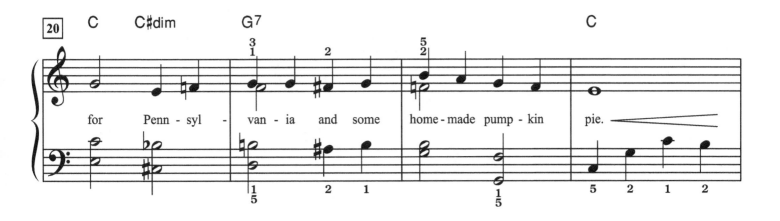

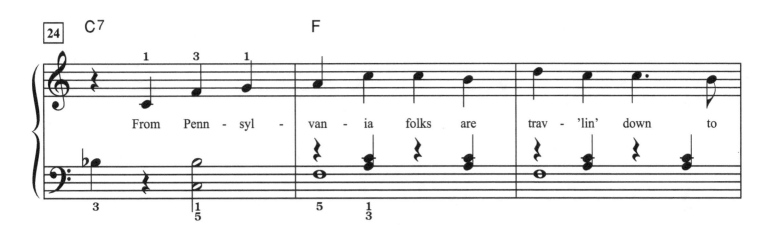

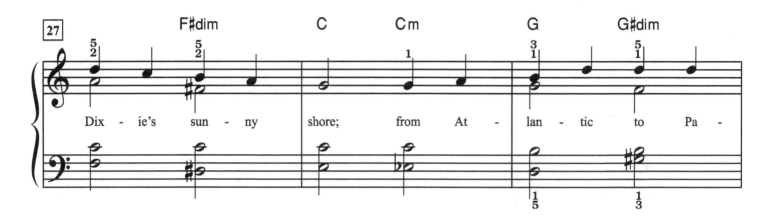

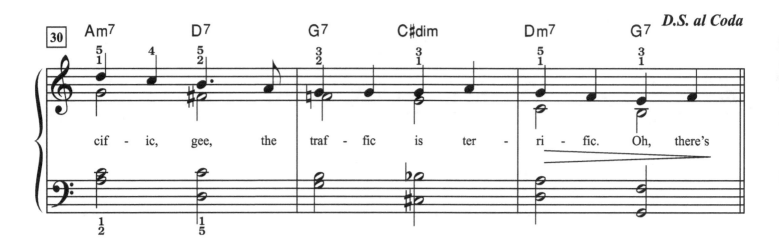

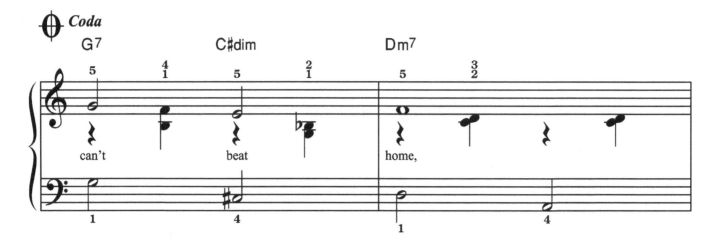

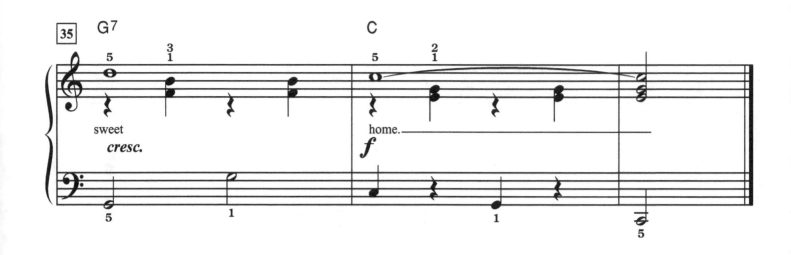

I'LL BE HOME FOR CHRISTMAS

Words by Kim Gannon
Music by Walter Kent
Arranged by Dan Coates

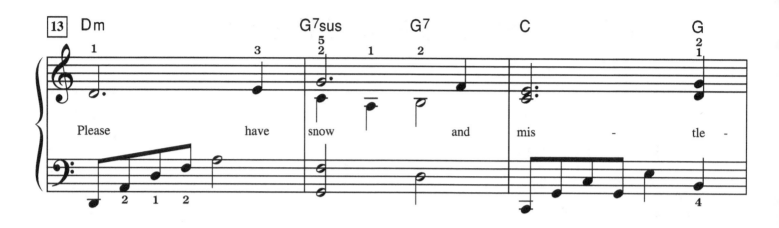

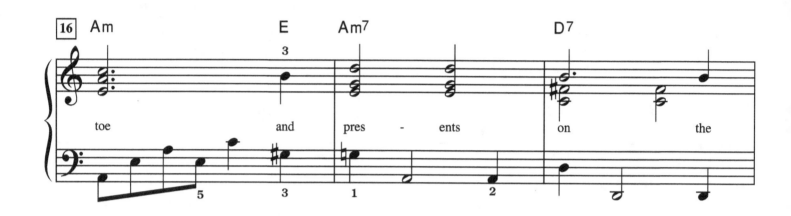

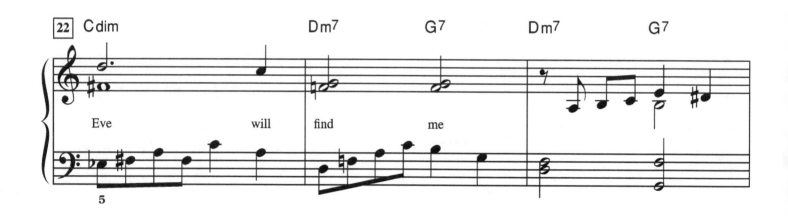

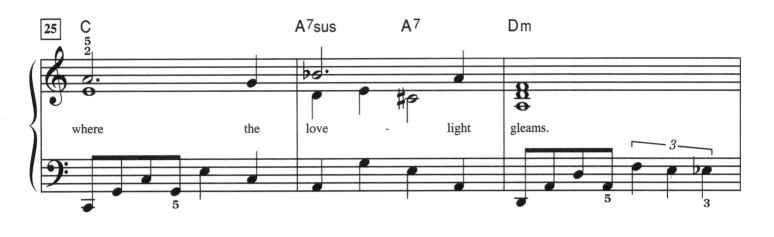

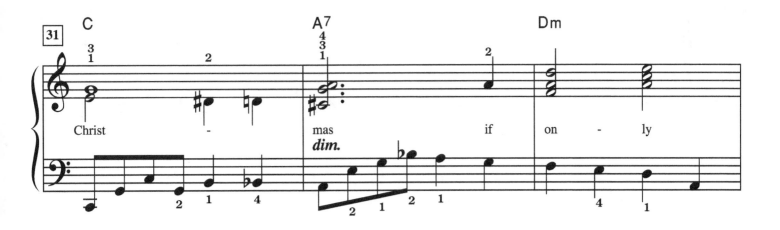

I SAW THREE SHIPS

Traditional Carol
Arranged by Dan Coates

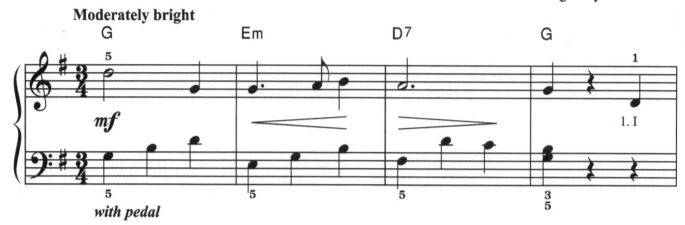

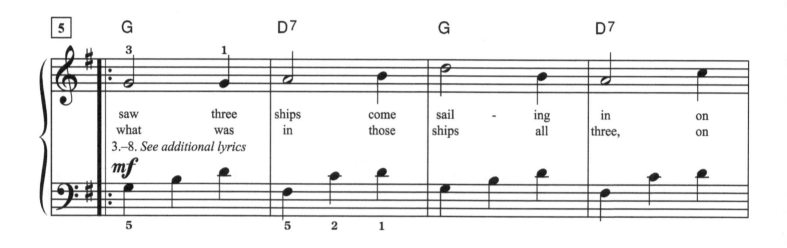

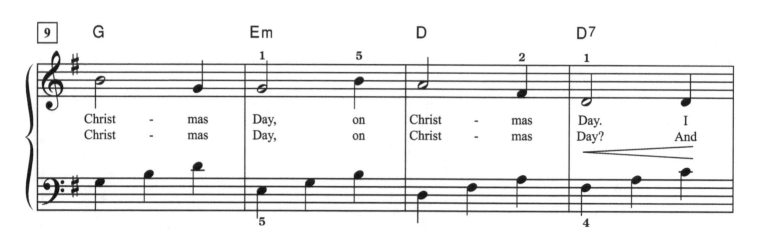

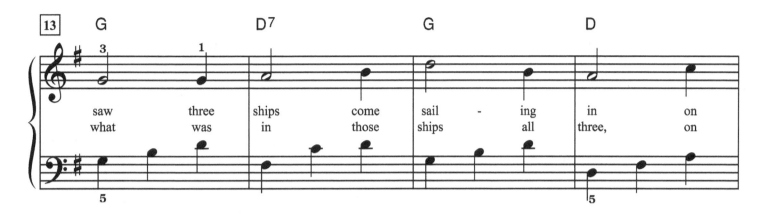

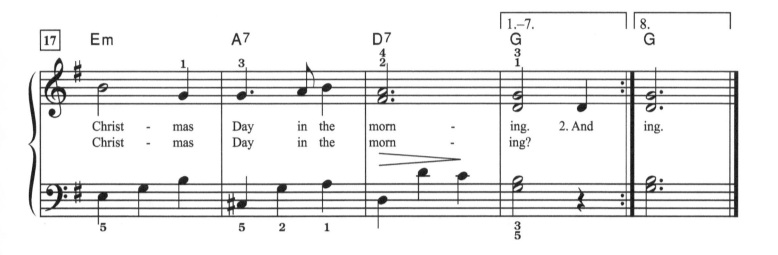

Verse 3:
The Virgin Mary and Christ were there,
On Christmas Day, on Christmas Day.
The Virgin Mary and Christ were there,
On Christmas Day in the morning.

Verse 4:
Pray, wither sailed those ships all three,
On Christmas Day, on Christmas Day?
Pray, wither sailed those ships all three,
On Christmas Day in the morning?

Verse 5:
O they sailed into Bethlehem,
On Christmas Day, on Christmas Day.
O they sailed into Bethlehem,
On Christmas Day in the morning.

Verse 6:
And all the bells on earth shall ring,
On Christmas day, on Christmas Day.
And all the bells on earth shall ring,
On Christmas Day in the morning.

Verse 7:
And all the angels in heaven shall sing,
On Christmas Day, on Christmas Day.
And all the angels in heaven shall sing,
On Christmas Day in the morning.

Verse 8:
Then let us all rejoice again,
On Christmas Day, on Christmas Day.
Then let us all rejoice again,
On Christmas Day in the morning.

IT CAME UPON THE MIDNIGHT CLEAR

Traditional Carol
Arranged by Dan Coates

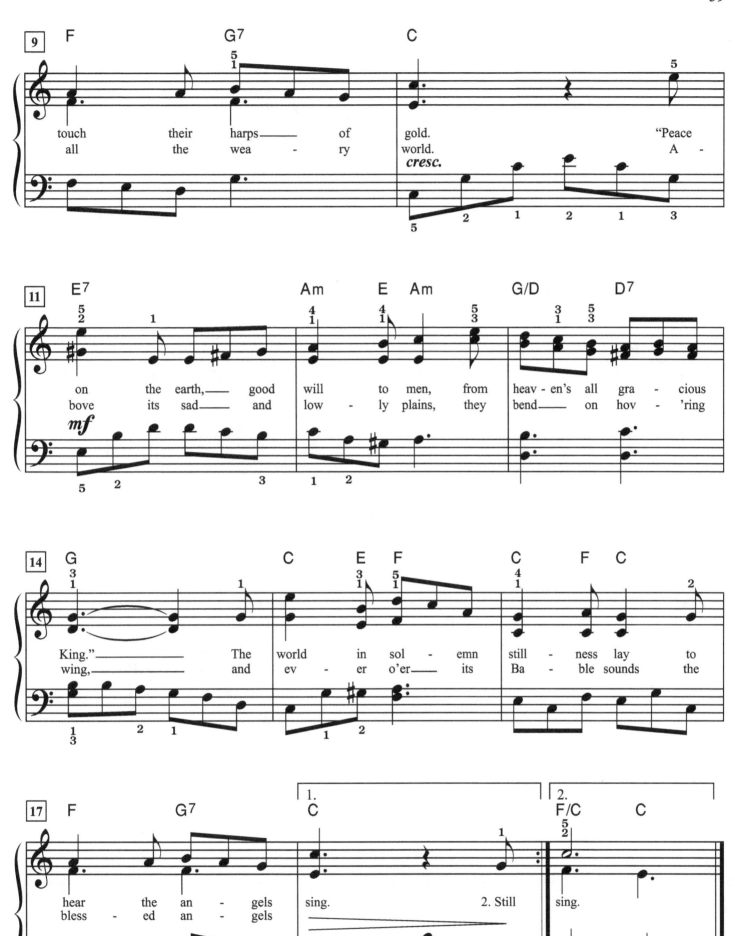

IT'S THE MOST
WONDERFUL TIME OF THE YEAR

Words and Music by
Eddie Pola and George Wyle
Arranged by Dan Coates

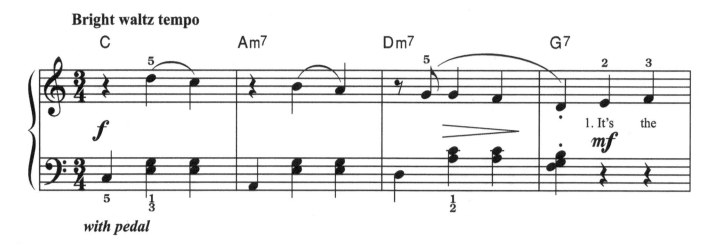

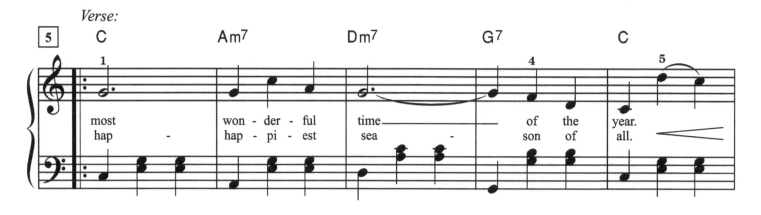

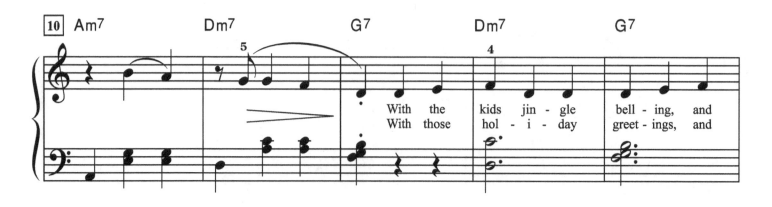

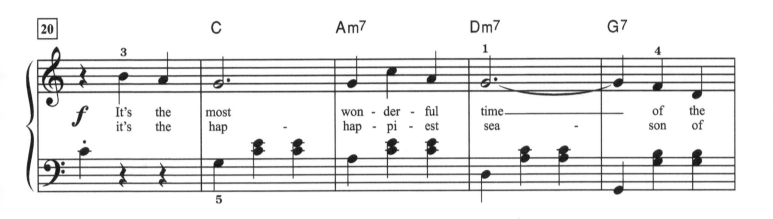

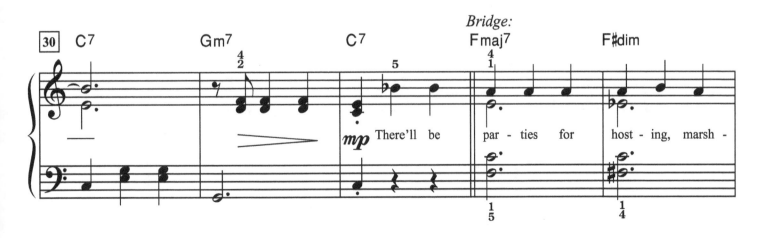

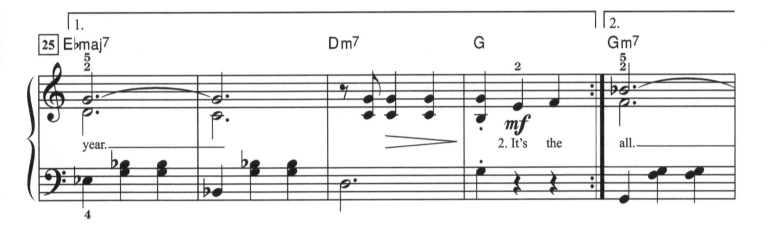

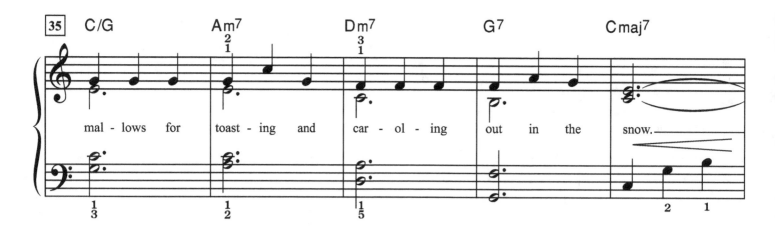

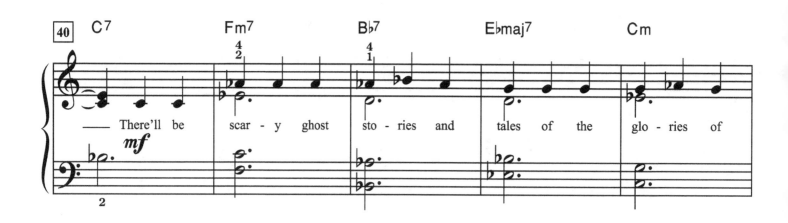

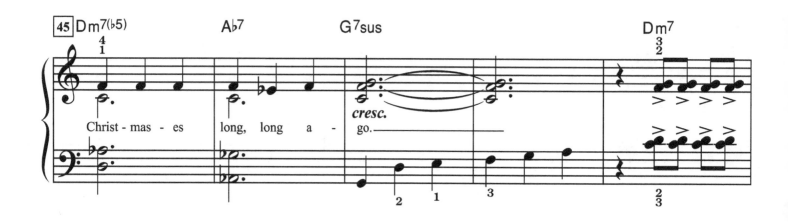

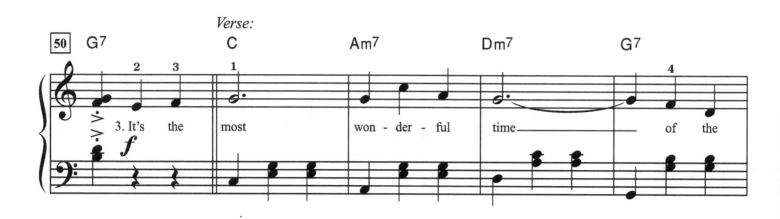

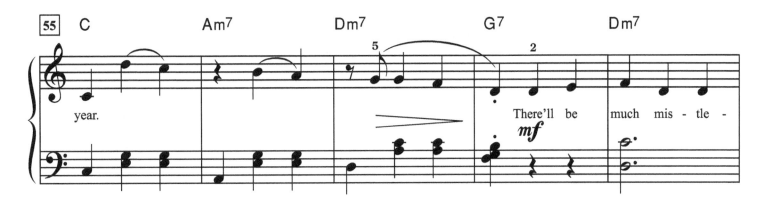

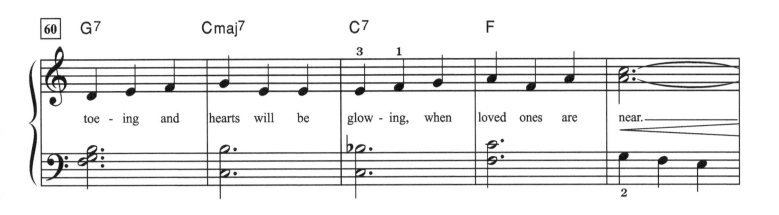

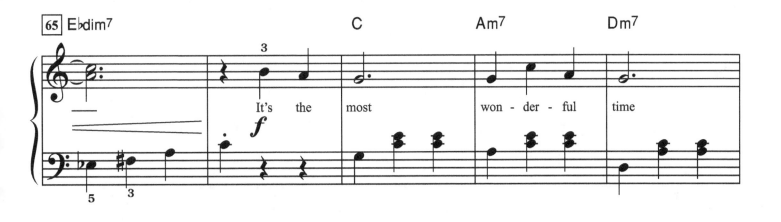

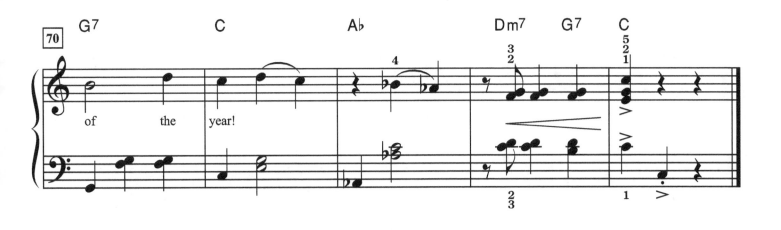

JINGLE BELLS

By James Pierpoint
Arranged by Dan Coates

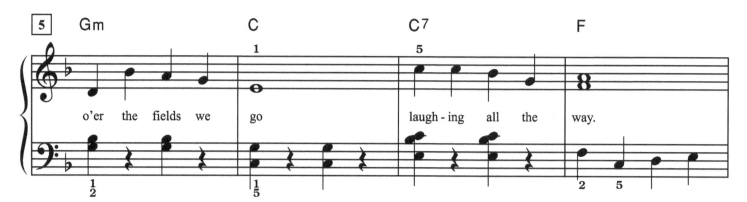

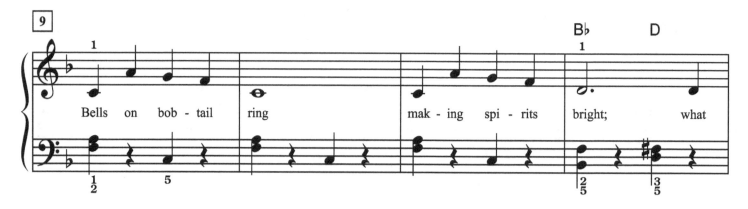

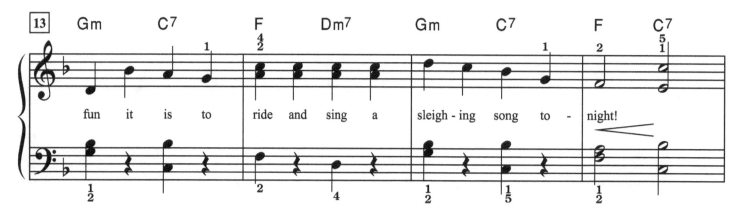

17 **F**

Jin - gle bells, jin - gle bells, jin - gle all the way.

f

3 1 5

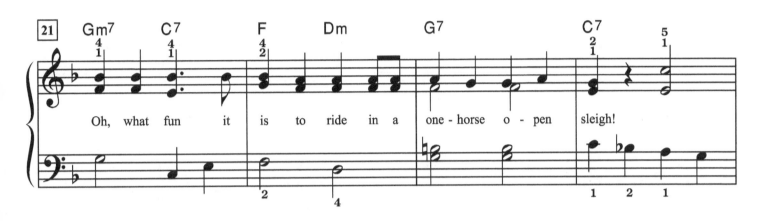

21 **Gm7** **C7** **F** **Dm** **G7** **C7**

Oh, what fun it is to ride in a one - horse o - pen sleigh!

2 4

1 2 1

25 **F**

Jin - gle bells, jin - gle bells, jin - gle all the way.

29 **Gm7** **C7** **F** **Dm** **Gm7** **C7** **F**

Oh, what fun it is to ride in a one - horse o - pen sleigh! *mp*

1 5

1 2 1 5

LET IT SNOW! LET IT SNOW! LET IT SNOW!

Words by Sammy Cahn
Music by Jule Styne
Arranged by Dan Coates

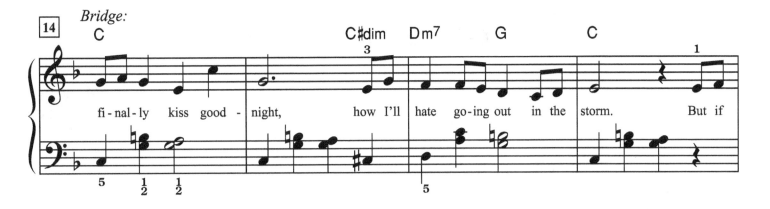

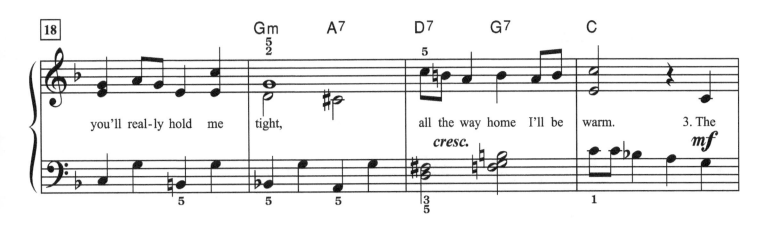

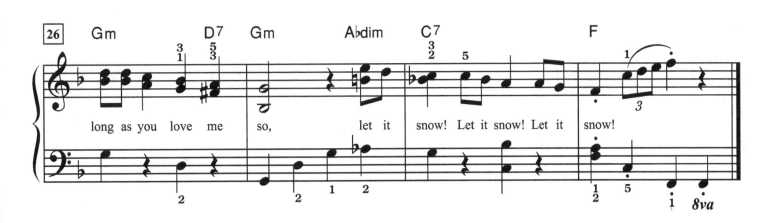

JINGLE BELL ROCK

Words and Music by
Joe Neal and Jim Boothe
Arranged by Dan Coates

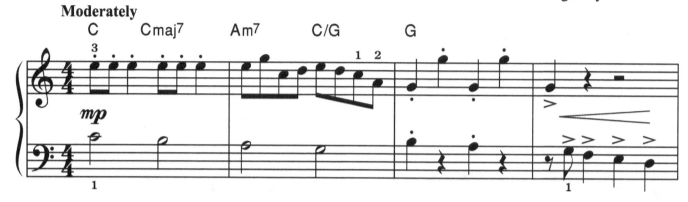

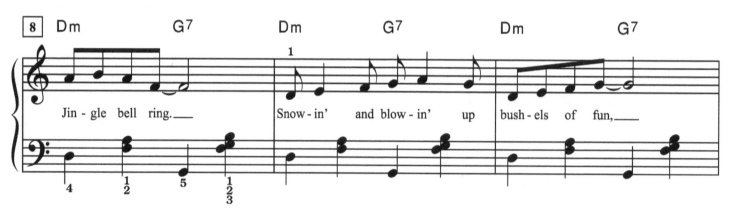

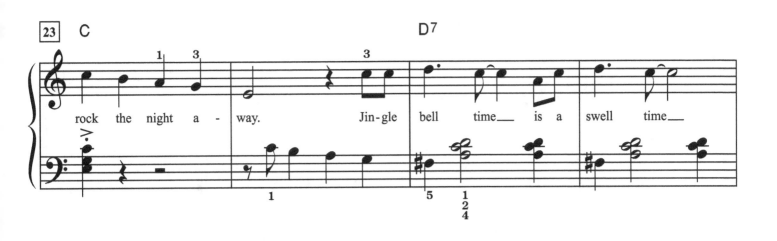

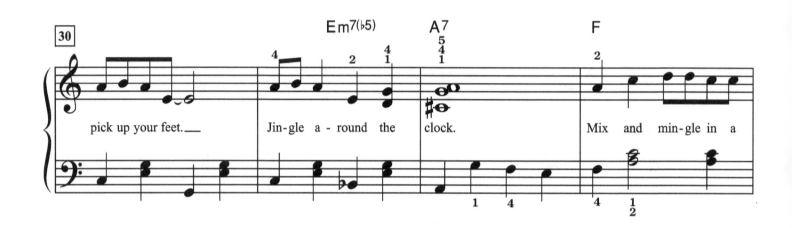

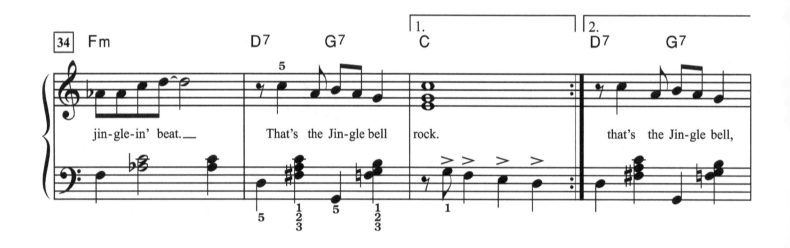

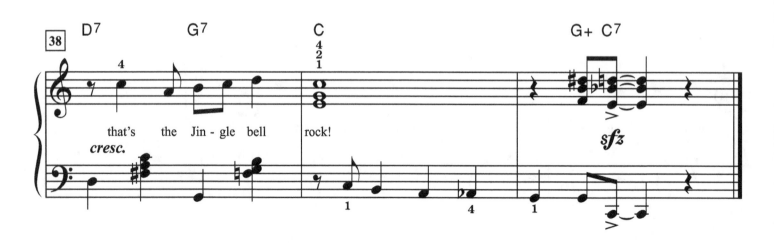

THE LITTLE DRUMMER BOY

Words and Music by Harry Simeone,
Henry Onorati and Katherine Davis
Arranged by Dan Coates

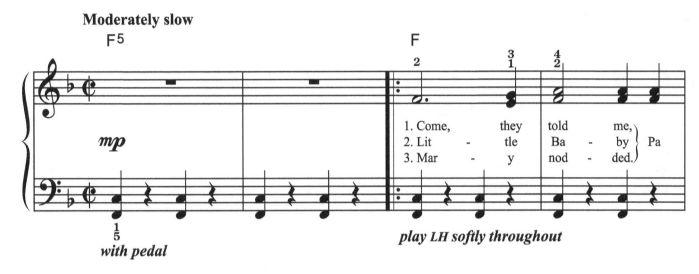

rum pum pum pum.

To lay be - fore the King,
That's fit to give our King,
I played my best for Him

the King, Pa

rum pum pum pum,　rum pum pum pum,　rum pum pum pum.

1., 2.

So to honor Him,
Shall I play for you?

Pa rum pum pum pum.

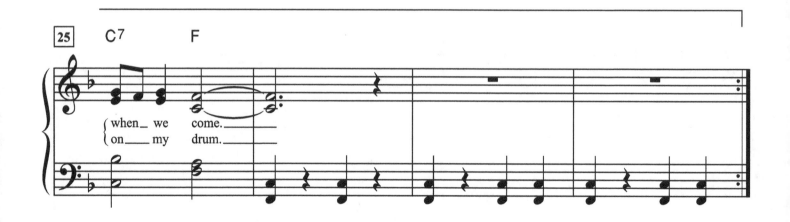

when we come.
on my drum.

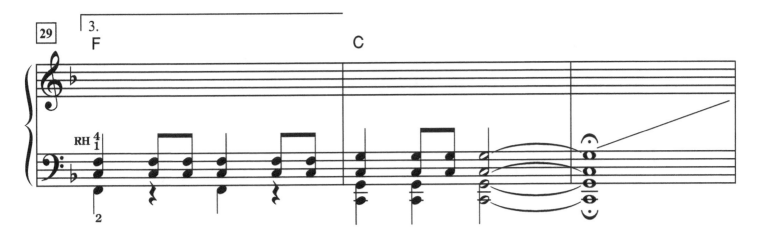

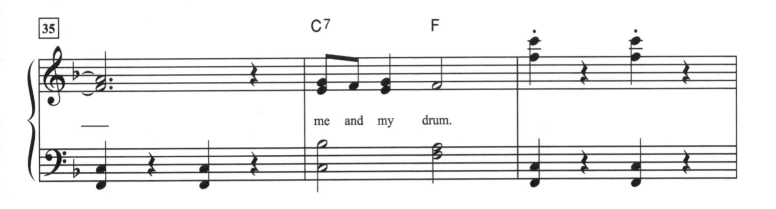

MERRY CHRISTISLAMAKWANZAKAH!

Words and Music by Brent Hardesty
Arranged by Dan Coates

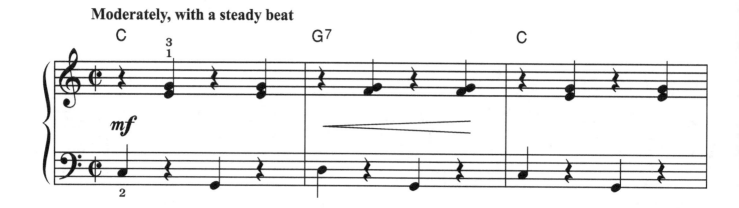

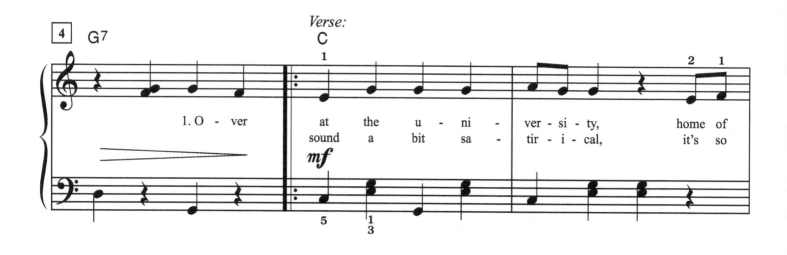

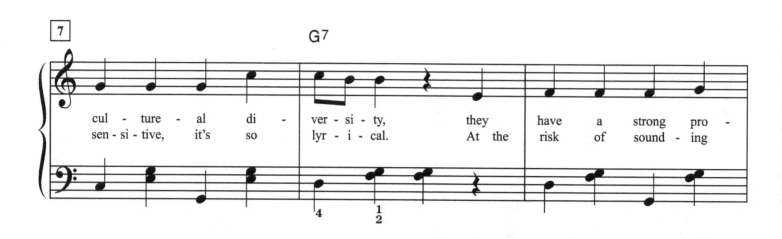

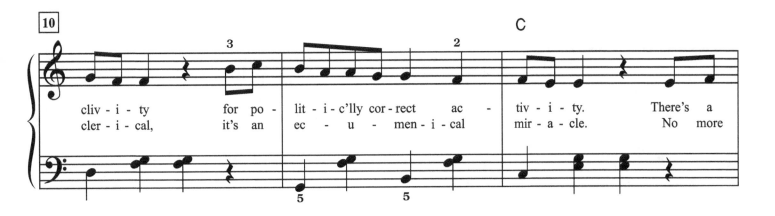

10 clivi-ty for po- lit-i-c'lly cor-rect ac- tiv-i-ty. There's a
cler-i-cal, it's an ec- u- men-i-cal mir-a-cle. No more

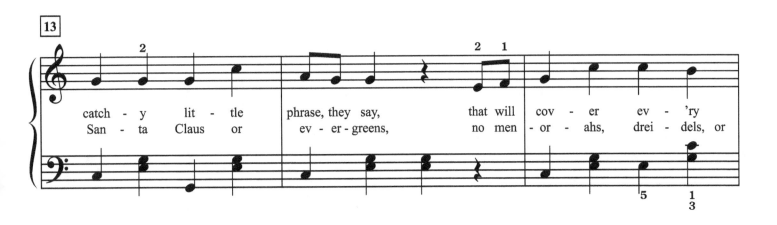

13 catch-y lit- tle phrase, they say, that will cov- er ev-'ry
San- ta Claus or ev- er-greens, no men -or-ahs, drei- dels, or

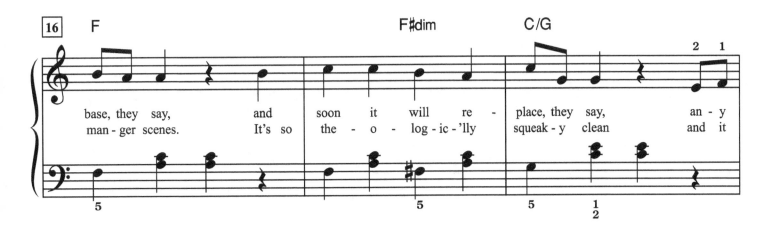

16 base, they say, and soon it will re- place, they say, an-y
man-ger scenes. It's so the- o- log-ic-'lly squeak-y clean and it

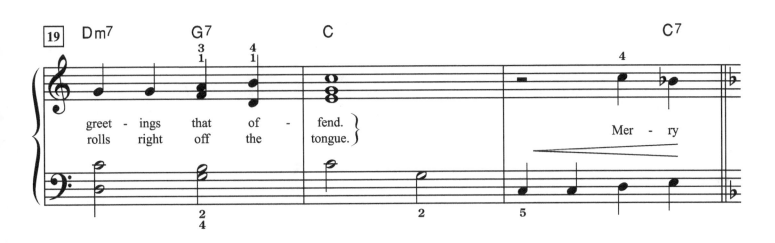

19 greet- ings that of- fend.
rolls right off of the tongue.

Mer- ry

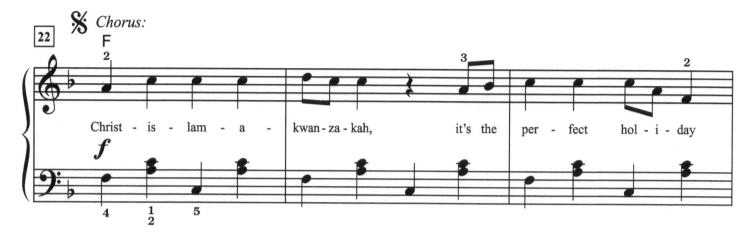

Chorus:

F

Christ - is - lam - a - kwan - za - kah, it's the per - fect hol - i - day

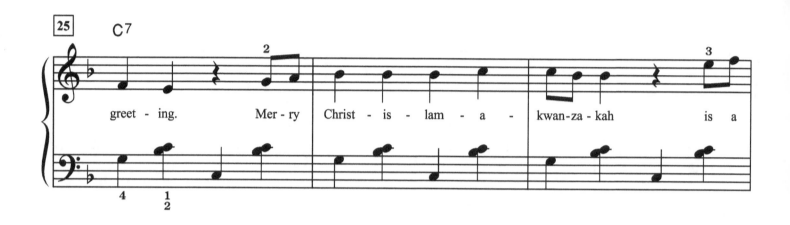

C7

greet - ing. Mer - ry Christ - is - lam - a - kwan - za - kah is a

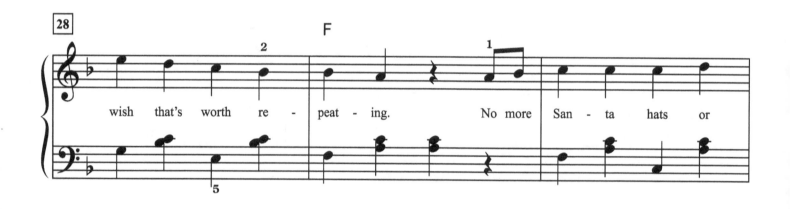

F

wish that's worth re - peat - ing. No more San - ta hats or

B♭

yar - mal - kes, no more "Deck the Halls" or "fa la la." Grab a

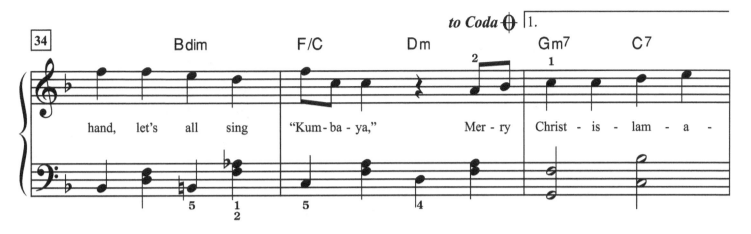

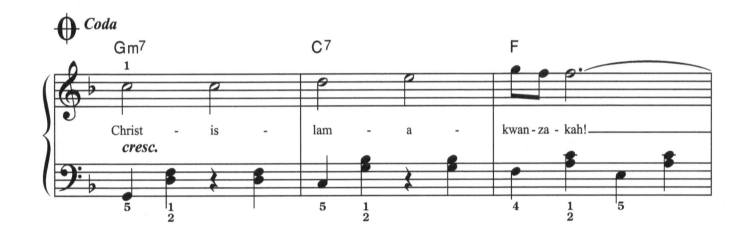

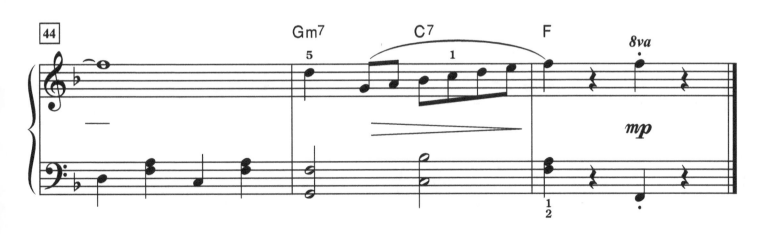

MISTLETOE AND HOLLY

Words and Music by Frank Sinatra,
Dok Stanford and Henry Sanicola
Arranged by Dan Coates

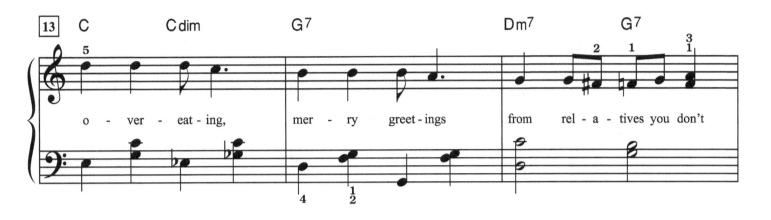

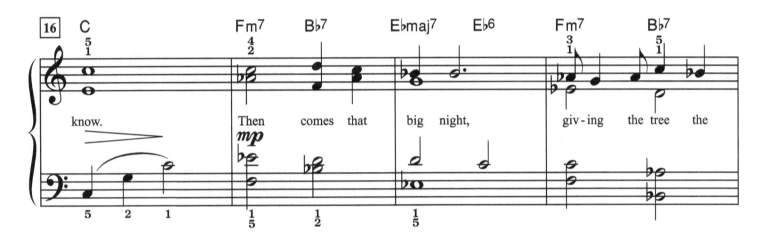

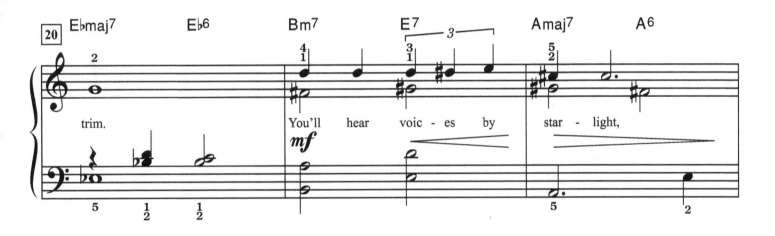

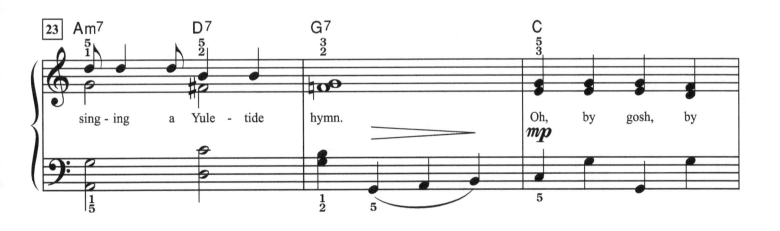

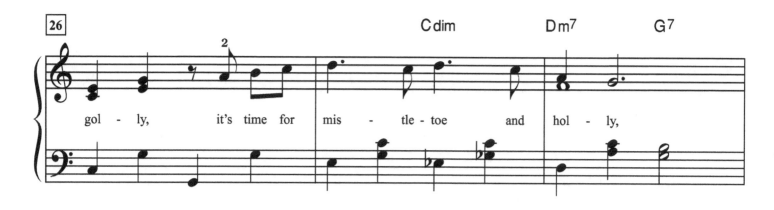

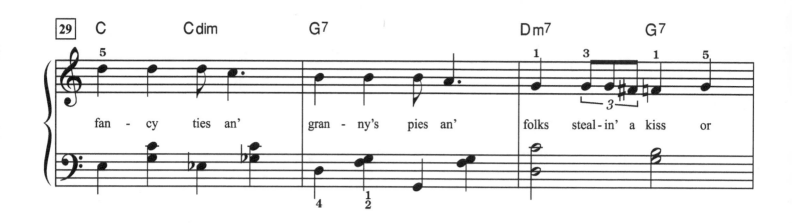

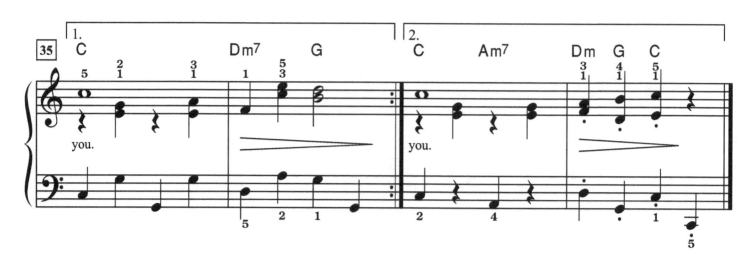

NUTTIN' FOR CHRISTMAS

Words and Music by
Sid Tepper and Roy C. Bennett
Arranged by Dan Coates

Chorus:

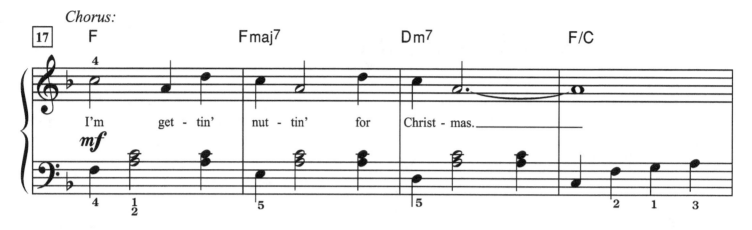

I'm get - tin' nut - tin' for Christ - mas.

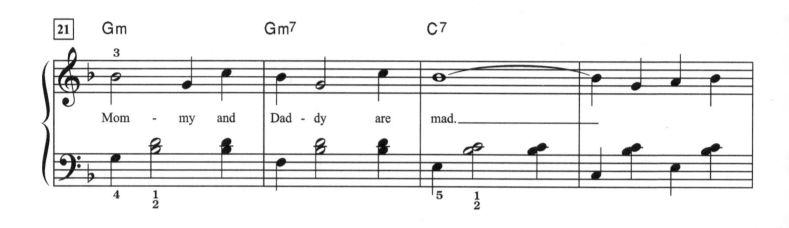

Mom - my and Dad - dy are mad.

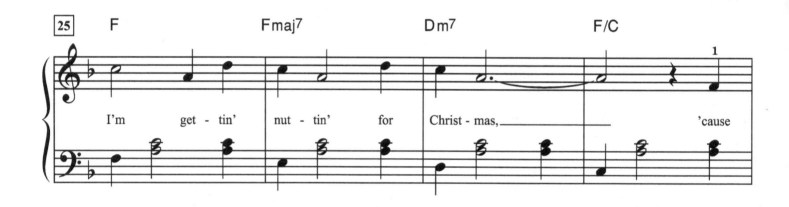

I'm get - tin' nut - tin' for Christ - mas,_____ 'cause

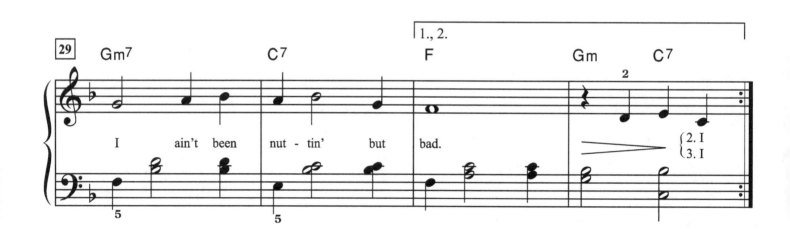

I ain't been nut - tin' but bad.

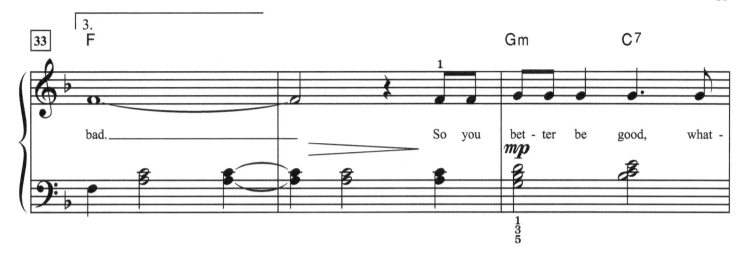

Verse 2:
I put a tack on teacher's chair;
Somebody snitched on me.
I tied a knot in Susie's hair;
Somebody snitched on me.
I did a dance on Mommy's plants,
Climbed a tree and tore my pants,
Filled the sugar bowl with ants;
Somebody snitched on me.
(To Chorus:)

Verse 3:
I won't be seeing Santa Claus;
Somebody snitched on me.
He won't come visit me because
Somebody snitched on me.
Next year I'll be going straight,
Next year I'll be good, just wait.
I'd start now but it's too late;
Somebody snitched on me.
(To Chorus:)

O CHRISTMAS TREE

Traditional Carol
Arranged by Dan Coates

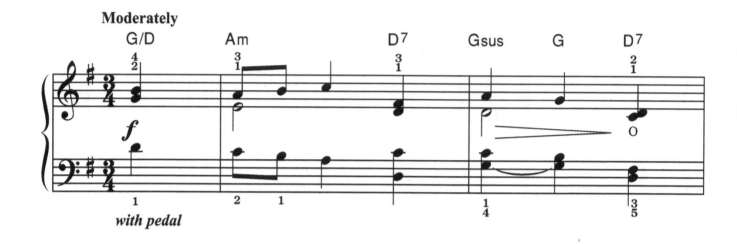

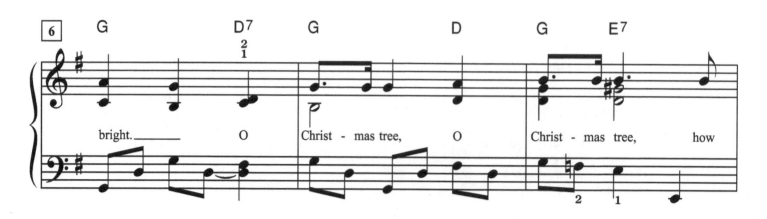

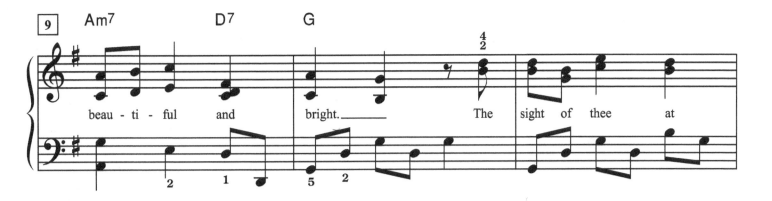

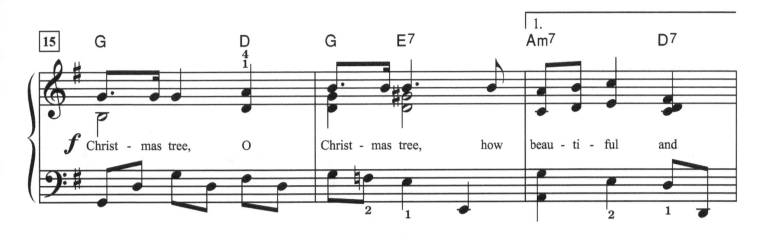

O COME, ALL YE FAITHFUL

Traditional Carol
Arranged by Dan Coates

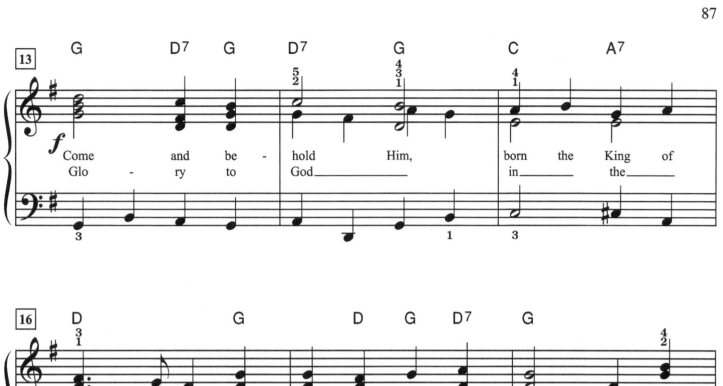

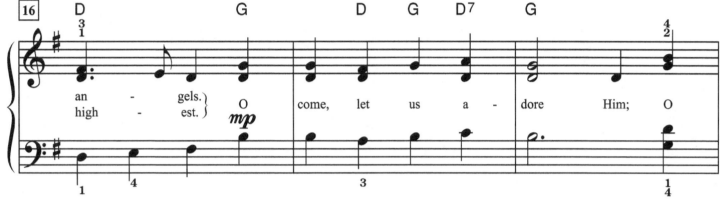

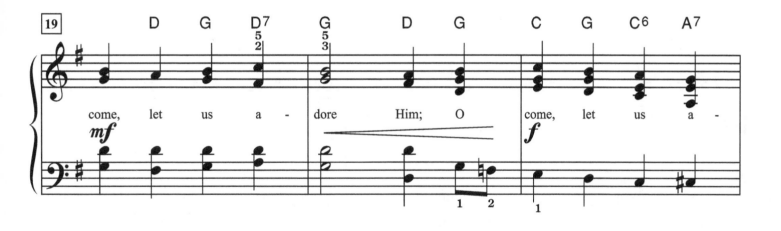

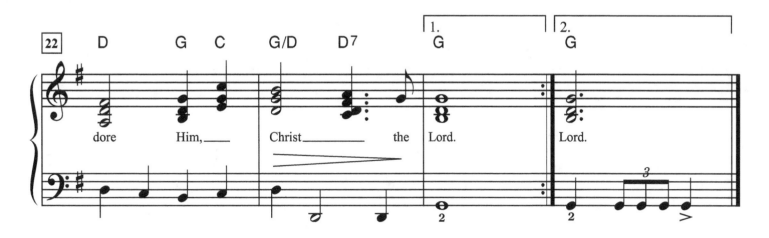

O COME, O COME EMMANUEL

English Lyrics by John M. Neale
Music: 13th Century Plainsong
Arranged by Dan Coates

O HOLY NIGHT

By John Dwight and Adolphe Adam
Arranged by Dan Coates

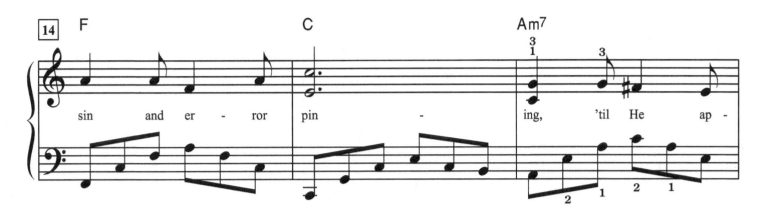

sin and er - ror pin - ing, 'til He ap -

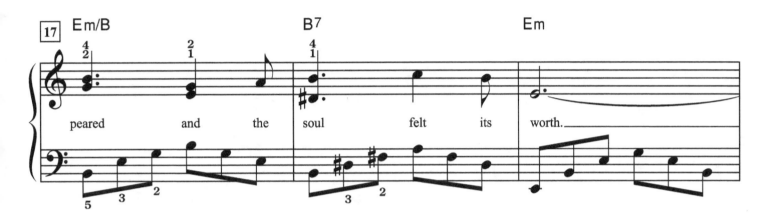

peared and the soul felt its worth.

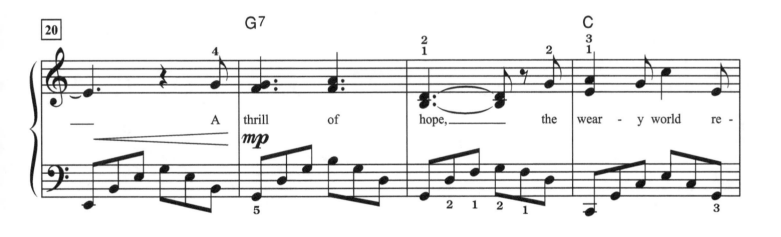

A thrill of hope, the wear - y world re -

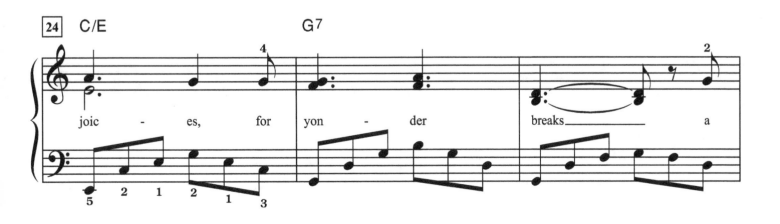

joic - es, for yon - der breaks a

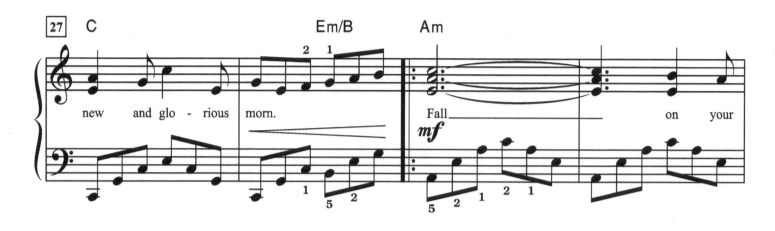

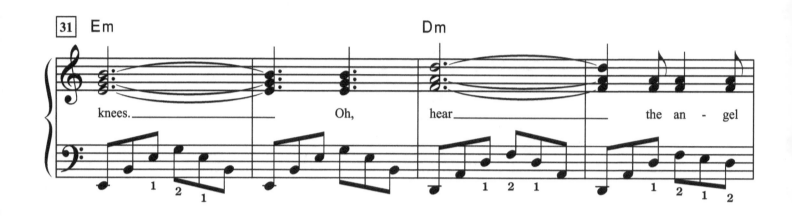

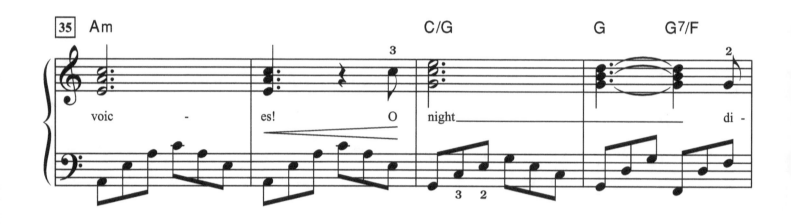

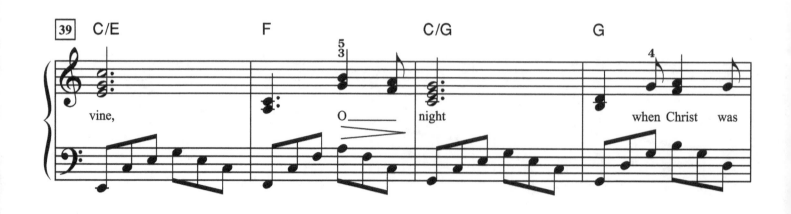

O LITTLE TOWN OF BETHLEHEM

By Phillips Brooks and Lewis Redner
Arranged by Dan Coates

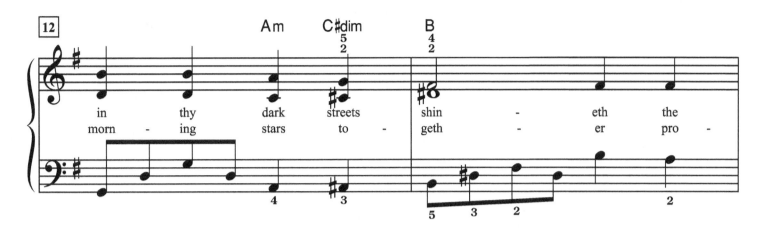

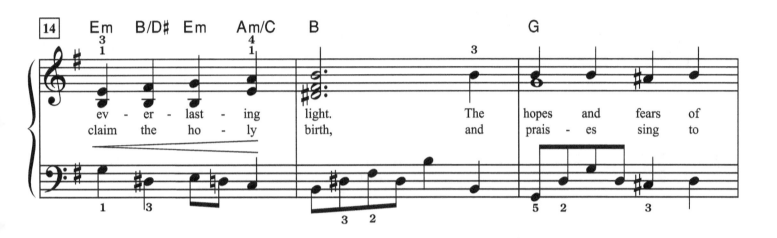

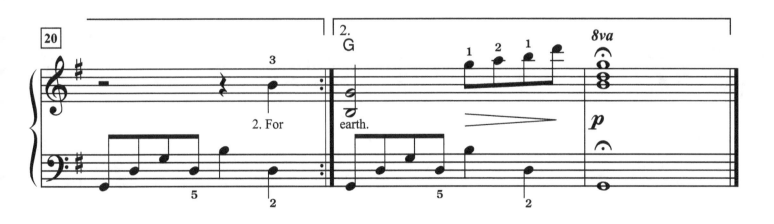

SANTA CLAUS IS COMIN' TO TOWN

Words by Haven Gillespie
Music by J. Fred Coots
Arranged by Dan Coates

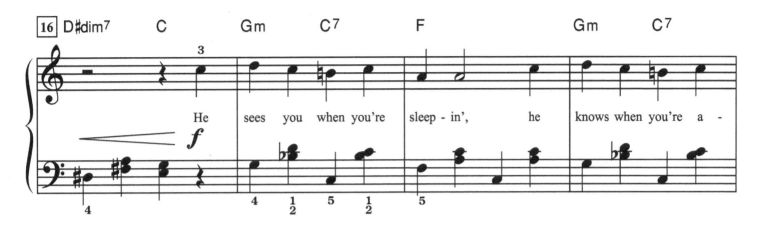

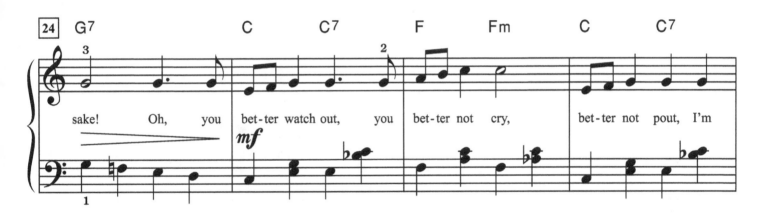

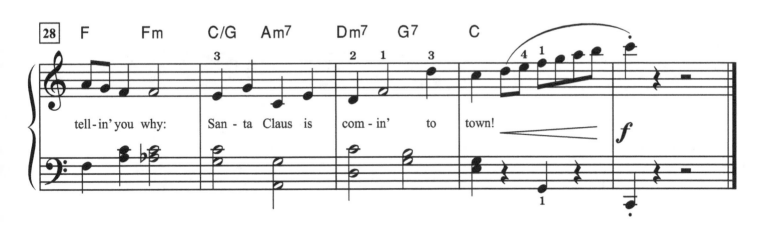

SANTA CLAUS ON DE COCONUT TREE

Words and Music by
John Fales and Horace Linsley
Arranged by Dan Coates

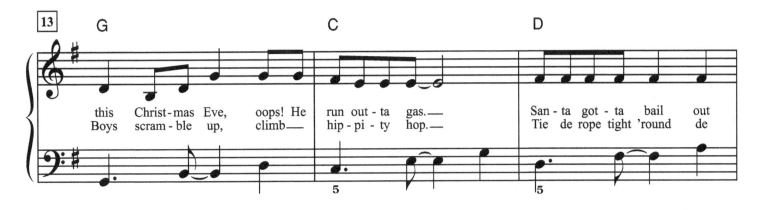

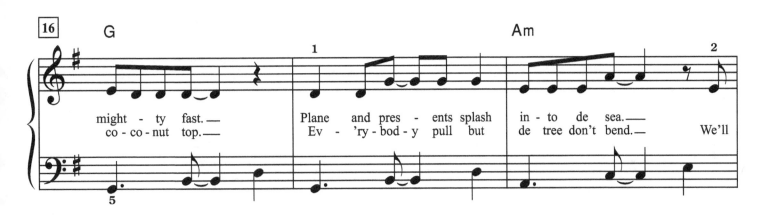

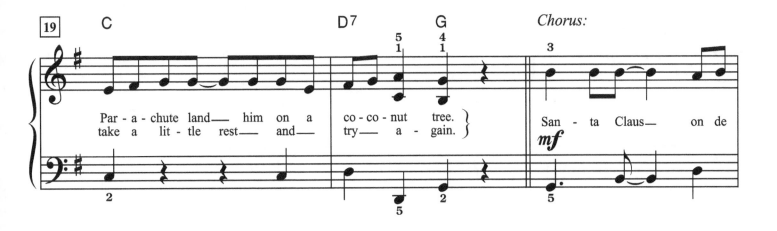

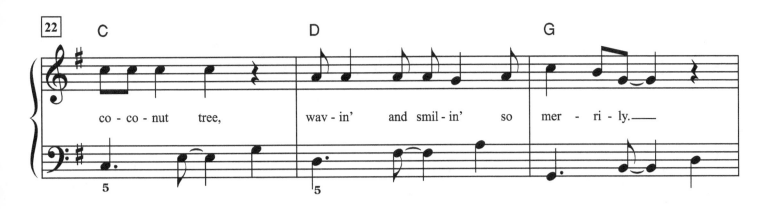

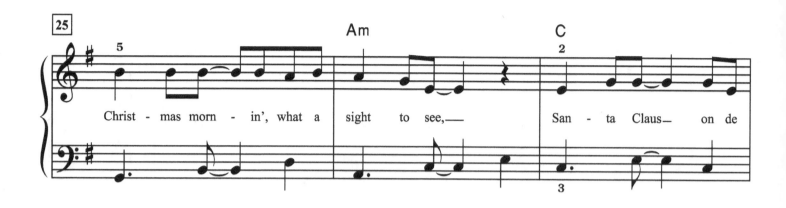

Christ - mas morn - in', what a sight to see,— San - ta Claus— on de

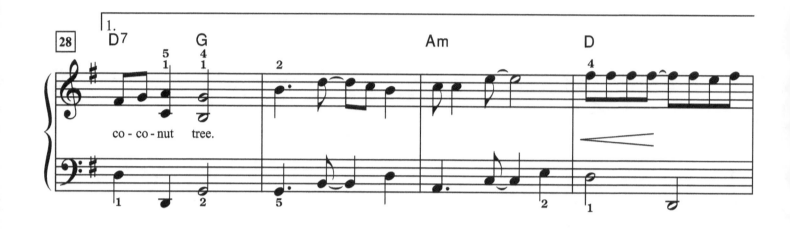

1.
co - co - nut tree.

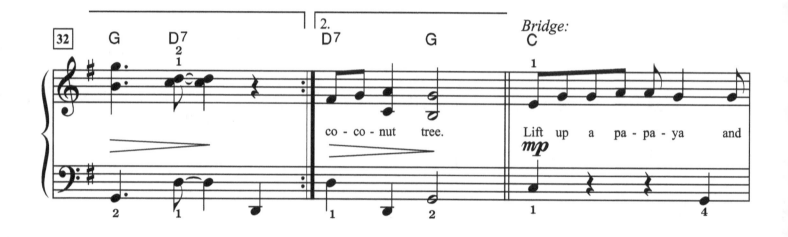

2.
co - co - nut tree.

Bridge:
Lift up a pa - pa - ya and

shrimp from the sea. Send good ol' San - ta sweet cin - na - mon tea.—

SLEIGH RIDE

By Leroy Anderson
Arranged by Dan Coates

Moderately bright

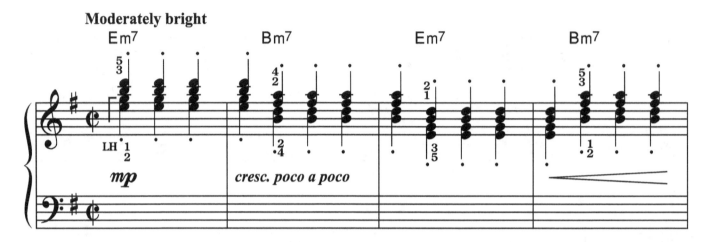

Verse:

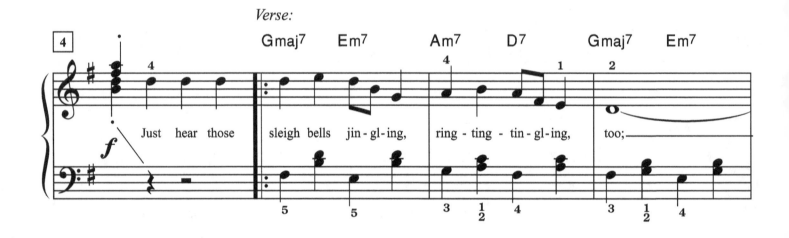

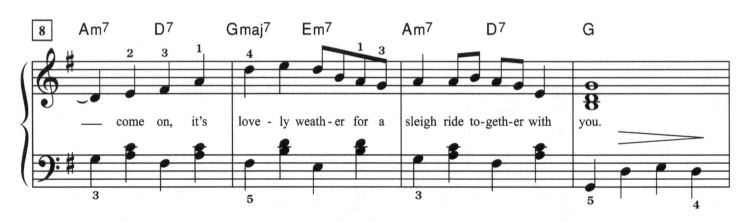

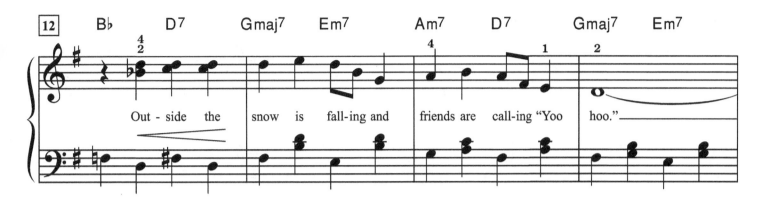

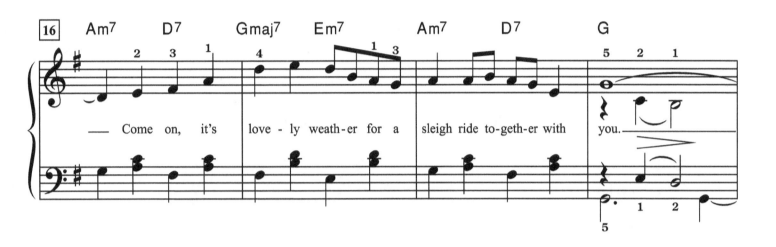

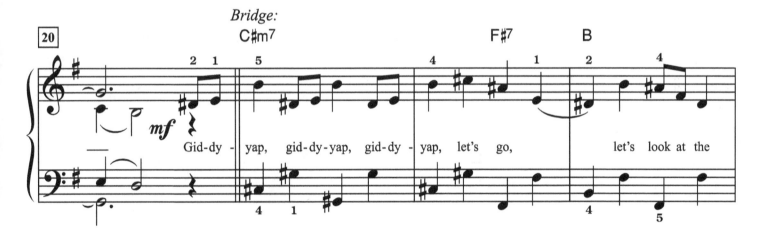

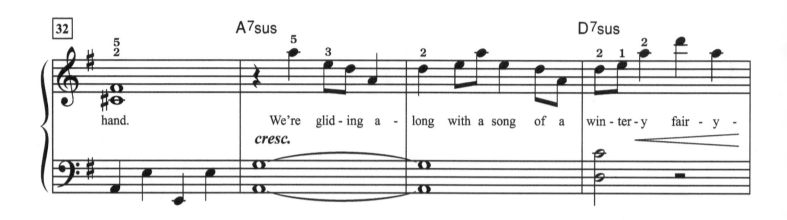

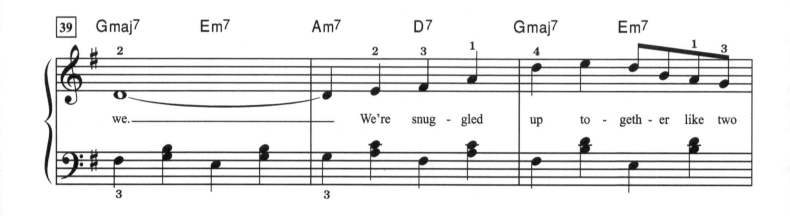

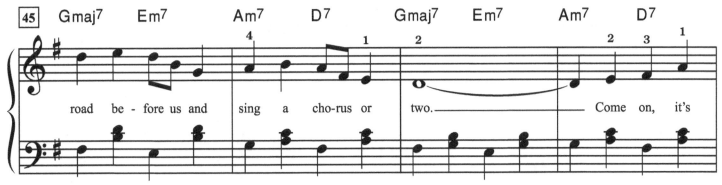

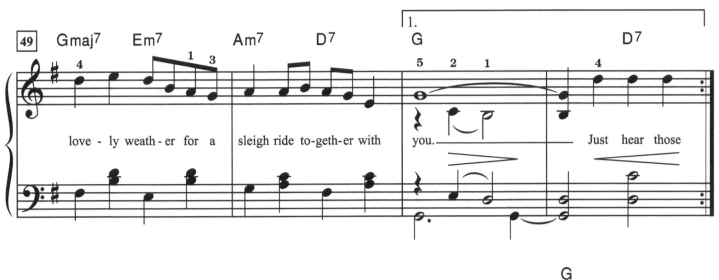

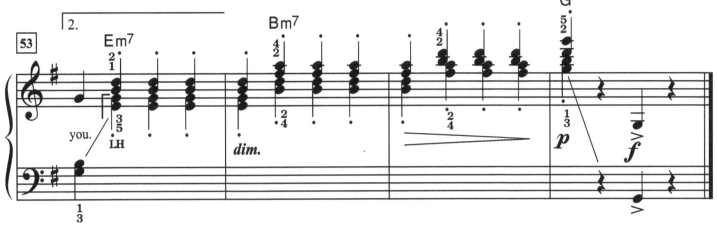

SILENT NIGHT

Words by Joseph Mohr
Music by Franz Grüber
Arranged by Dan Coates

108

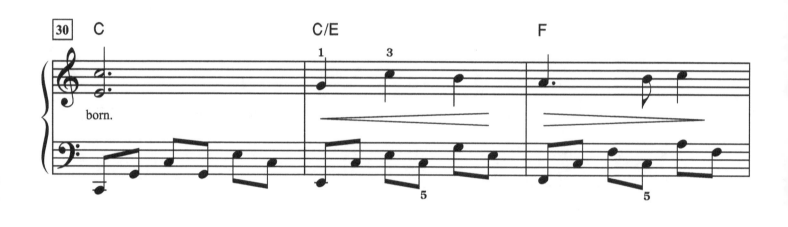

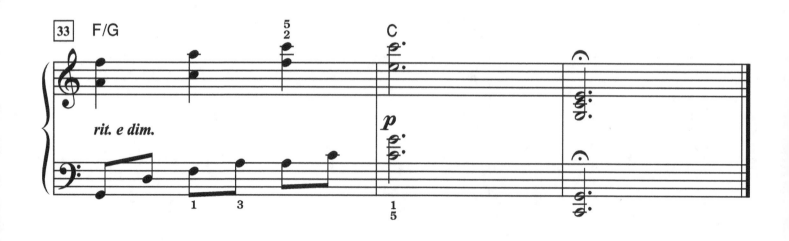

SUZY SNOWFLAKE

Words and Music by
Sid Tepper and Roy C. Bennett
Arranged by Dan Coates

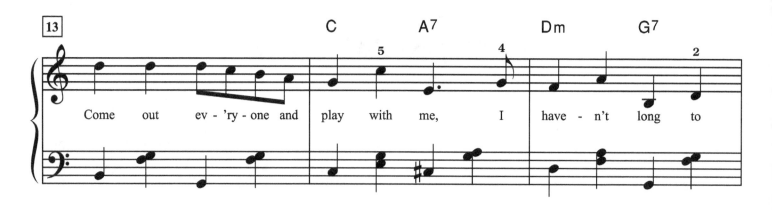

Come out ev - 'ry - one and play with me, I have - n't long to

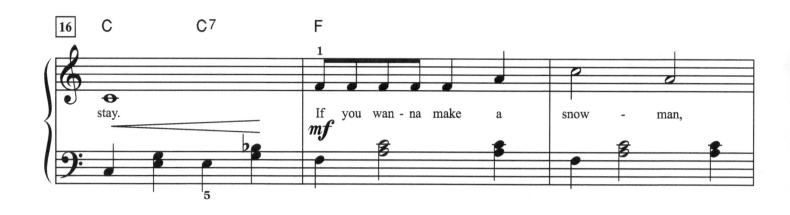

stay. *mf* If you wan - na make a snow - man,

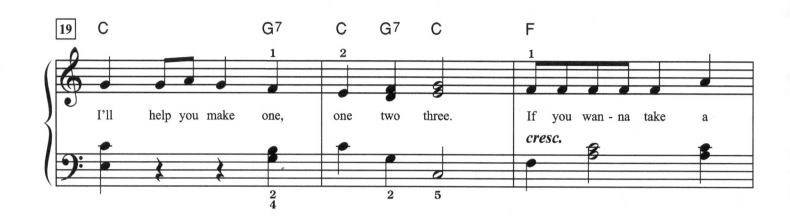

I'll help you make one, one two three. *cresc.* If you wan - na take a

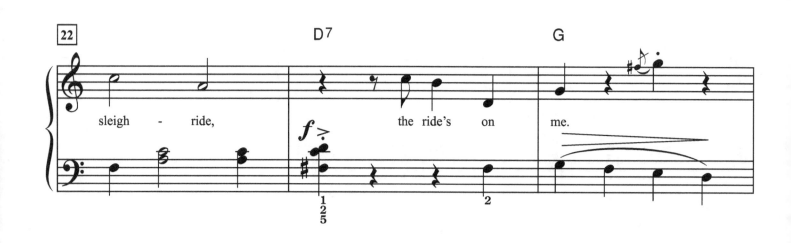

sleigh - ride, *f* the ride's on me.

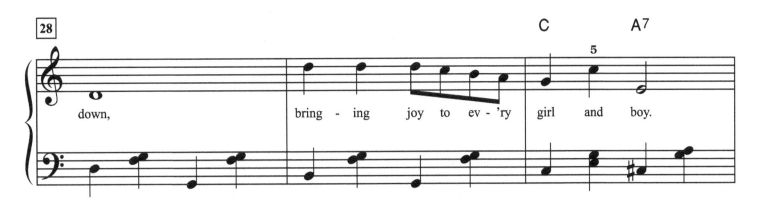

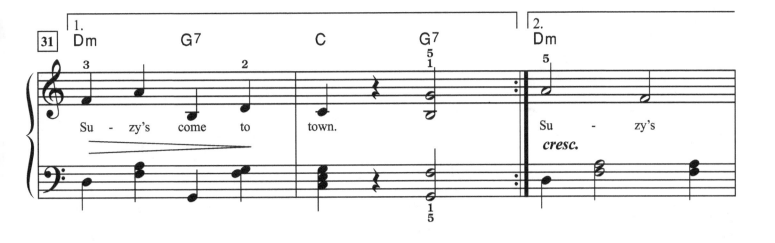

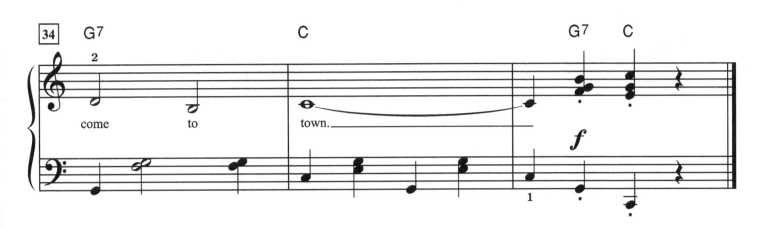

THERE IS NO CHRISTMAS
LIKE A HOME CHRISTMAS

Lyric by Carl Sigman
Music by Mickey J. Addy
Arranged by Dan Coates

114

26 D7 Dm7 A7 Dm7 G

fol - low them, you've been a - way too long. There is *mp*

29 C C7 F

no Christ - mas like a home

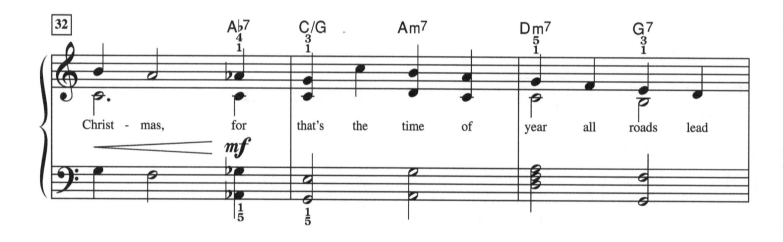

32 Ab7 C/G Am7 Dm7 G7

Christ - mas, for that's the time of year all roads lead *mf*

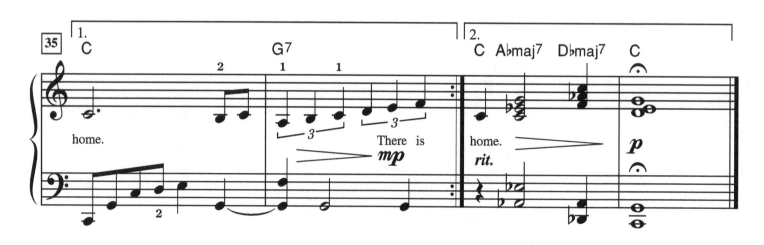

35 1. C G7 2. C Abmaj7 Dbmaj7 C

home. There is home. *p*
mp *rit.*

THIRTY-TWO FEET AND EIGHT LITTLE TAILS

Words and Music by John Redmond,
James Cavanaugh and Frank Weldon
Arranged by Dan Coates

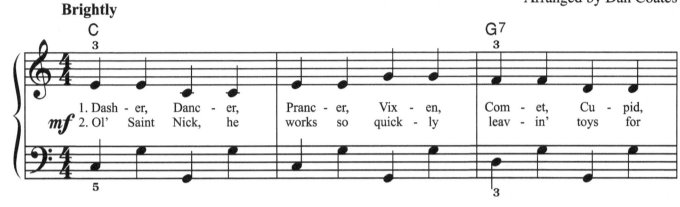

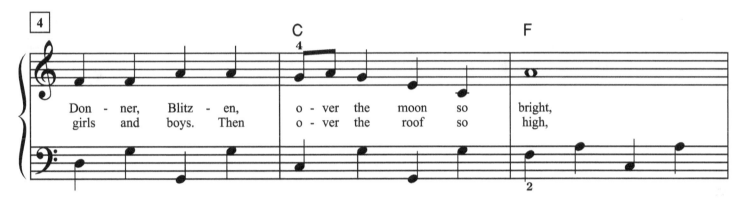

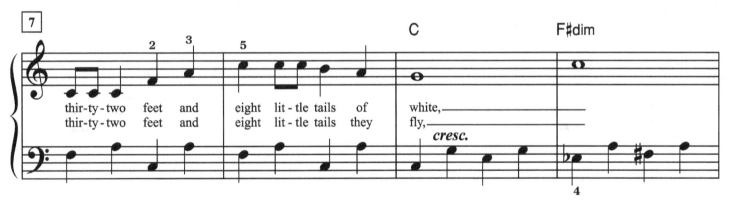

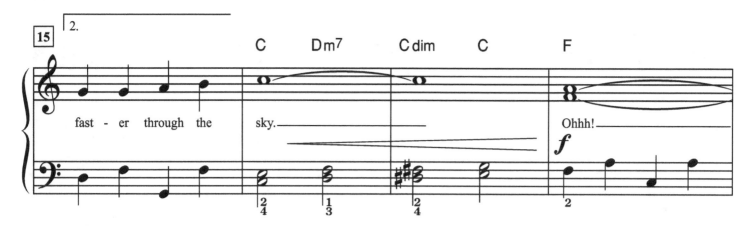

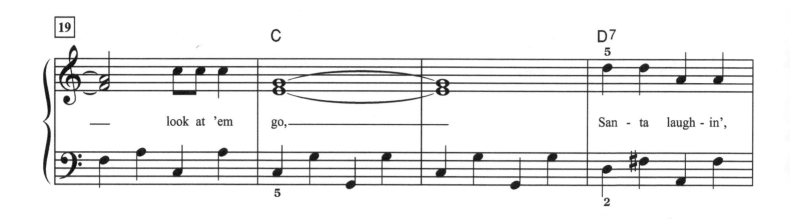

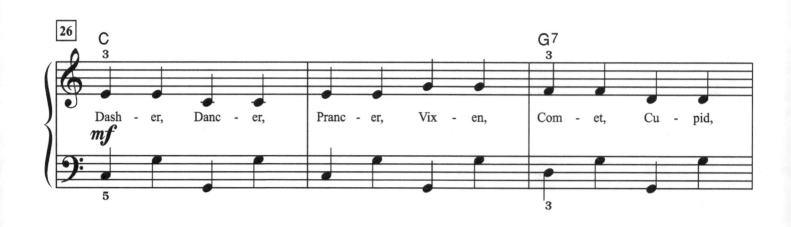

117

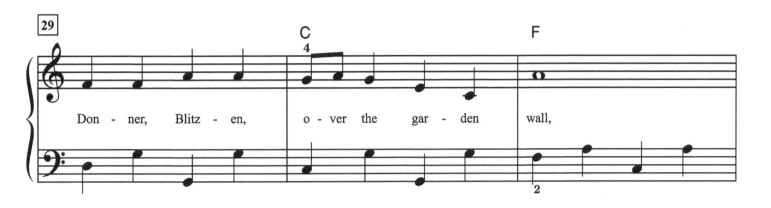

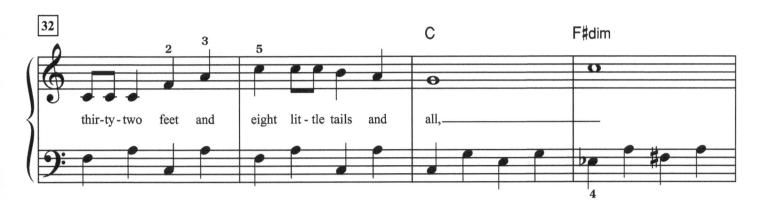

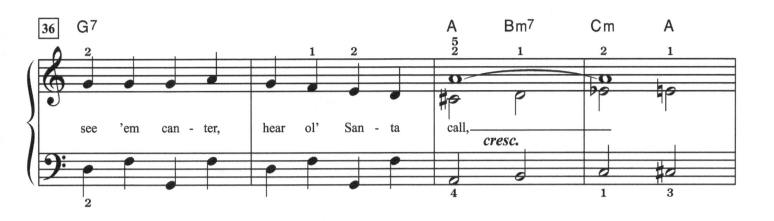

THESE ARE THE SPECIAL TIMES

Words and Music by Diane Warren
Arranged by Dan Coates

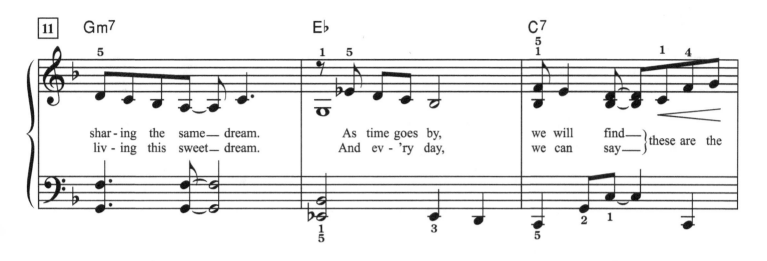

TOYLAND

Words by Glen MacDonough
Music by Victor Herbert
Arranged by Dan Coates

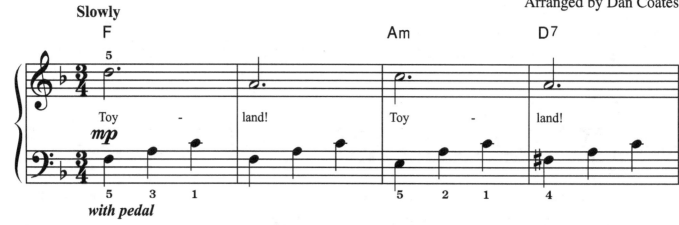

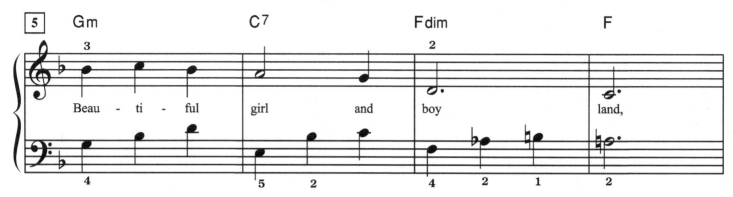

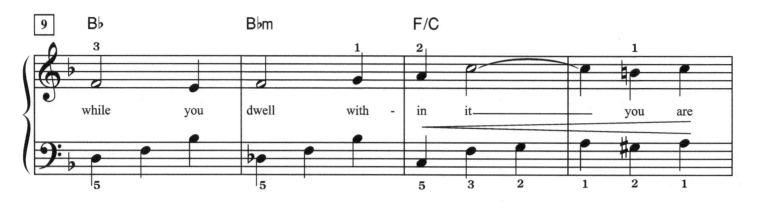

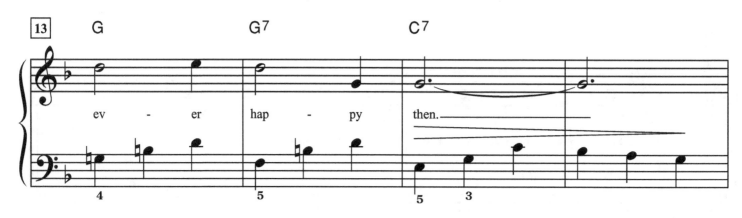

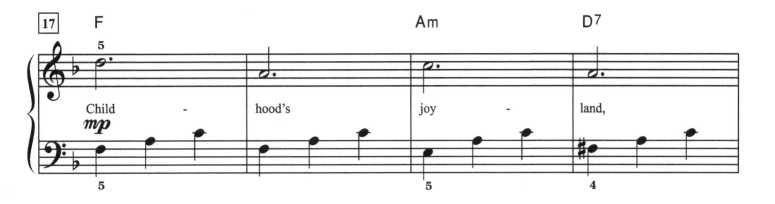

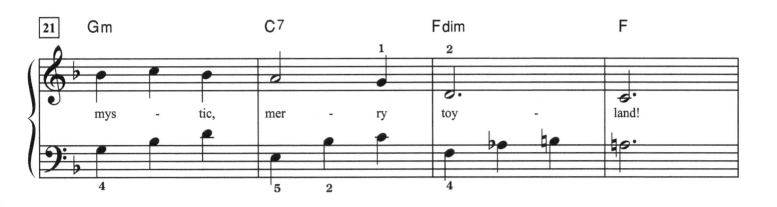

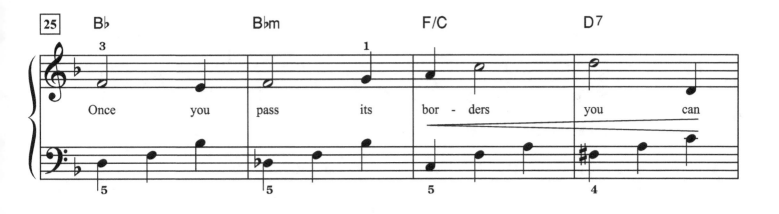

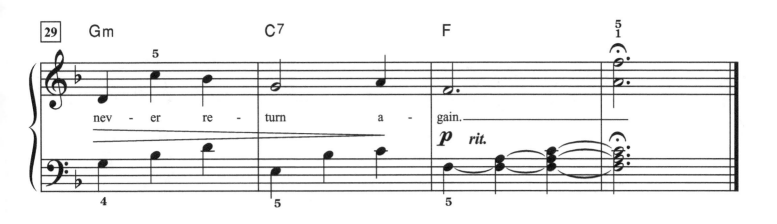

THE TWELVE DAYS OF CHRISTMAS

Traditional Carol
Arranged by Dan Coates

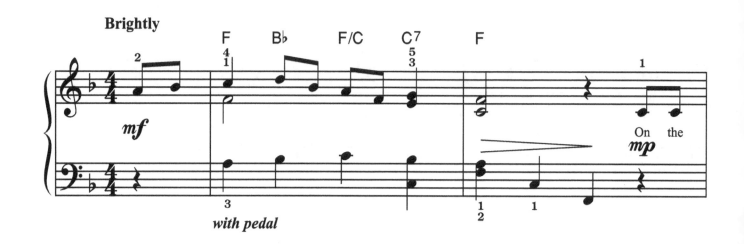

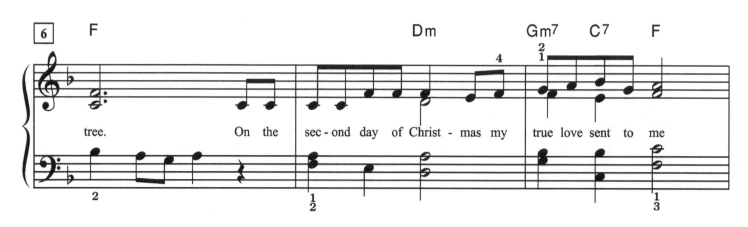

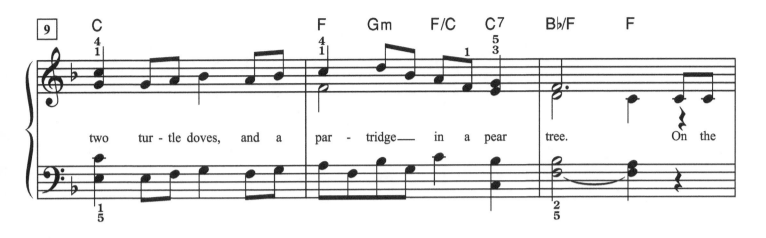

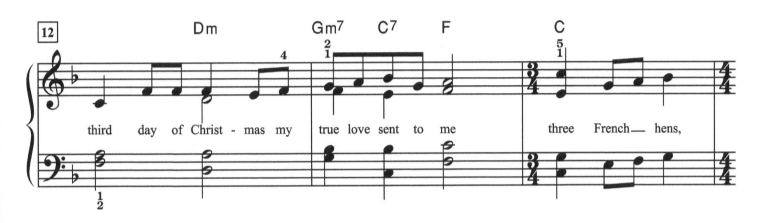

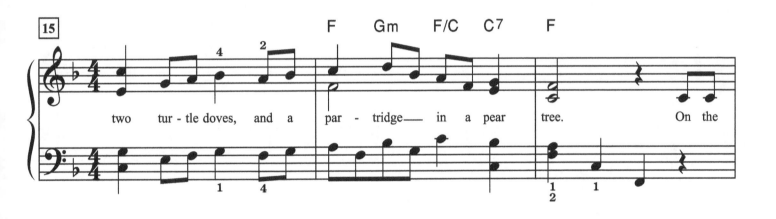

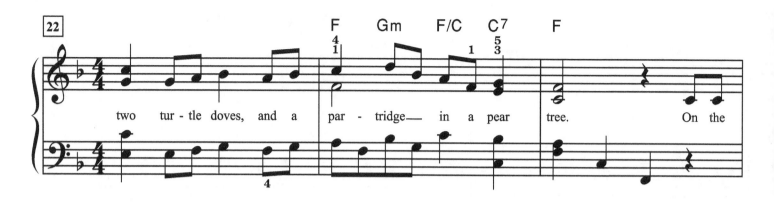

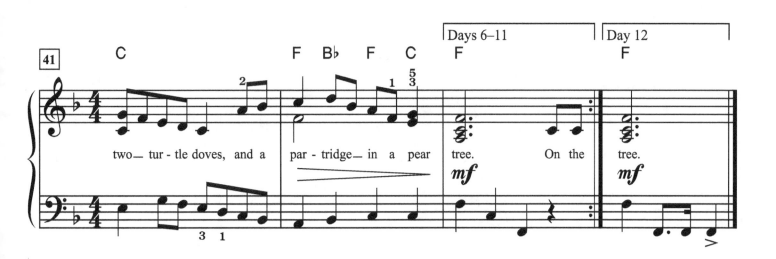

THE TWELVE POUNDS OF CHRISTMAS

Words and Music by Tom Zigler
Arranged by Dan Coates

butt still looks good— to me. On the sev - enth pound of Christ - mas my
(See additional verses)

un - cle said to me, Don't go back for sec - onds. Cut back just a lit - tle. The

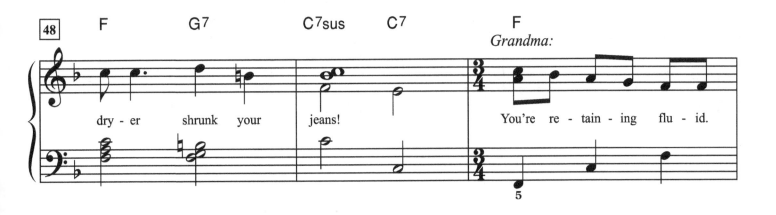

dry - er shrunk your jeans! You're re - tain - ing flu - id.

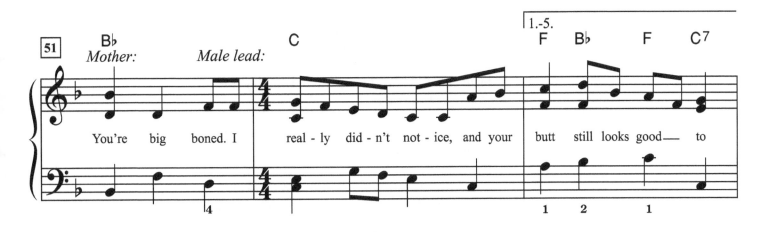

You're big boned. I real - ly did - n't not - ice, and your butt still looks good— to

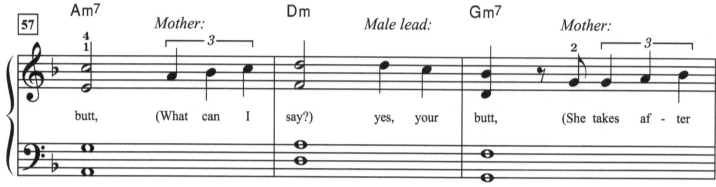

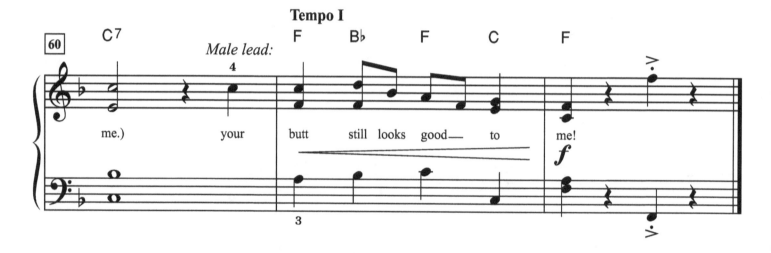

Additional verses:

On the eighth pound of Christmas my sister said to me,
That's not on Weight Watchers. *(etc.)*

On the ninth pound of Christmas my cousin said to me,
I wouldn't wear that Spandex. *(etc.)*

On the tenth pound of Christmas my brother said to me,
Schedule liposuction. *(etc.)*

On the eleventh pound of Christmas my nephew said to me,
Grazing is for cattle. *(etc.)*

On the twelfth pound of Christmas my mirror said to me,
Sooie, pig, sooie! *(etc.)*

UP ON THE HOUSETOP

Words and Music by
Benjamin Hanby
Arranged by Dan Coates

WE WISH YOU A MERRY CHRISTMAS

Traditional Carol
Arranged by Dan Coates

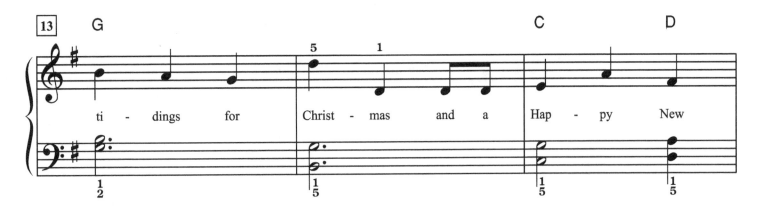

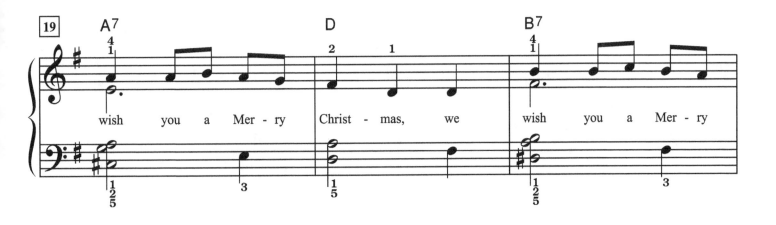

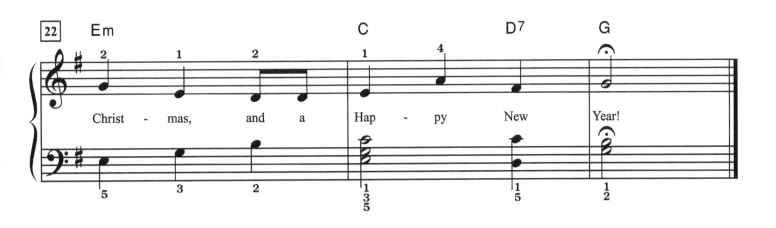

WHAT CHILD IS THIS?

Traditional Carol
Arranged by Dan Coates

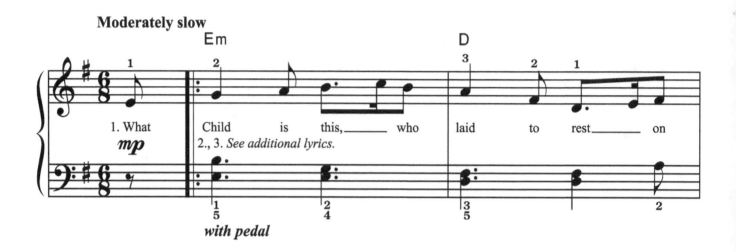

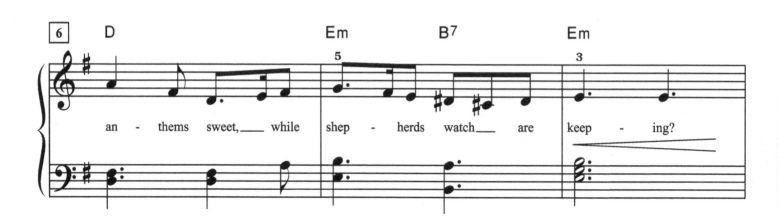

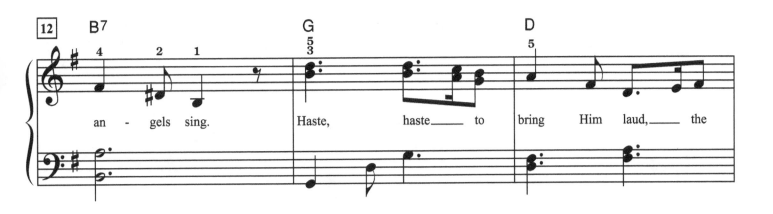

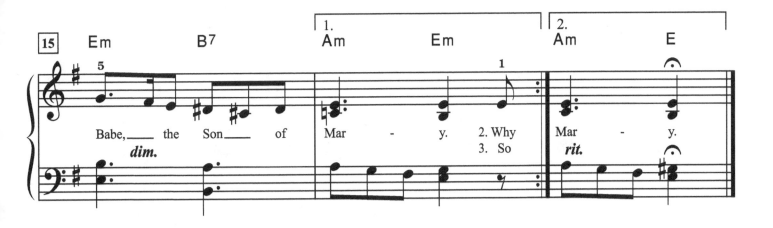

2. Why lies He in such mean estate,
   Where ox and ass are feeding?
   Good Christian fear, for sinners here
   The silent word is pleading.
   Nails, spear shall pierce Him through;
   The Cross be born for me, for you,
   Hail, hail the word made flesh,
   The Babe, the Son of Mary.

3. So bring Him incense, gold and myrrh,
   Come peasant, king to own Him.
   The King of Kings salvation brings;
   Let loving hearts enthrone Him.
   Raise, raise the song on high
   The Virgin sings her lullaby;
   Joy, joy for Christ is born.
   The Babe, the Son of Mary.

WE THREE KINGS OF ORIENT ARE

By John H. Hopkins, Jr.
Arranged by Dan Coates

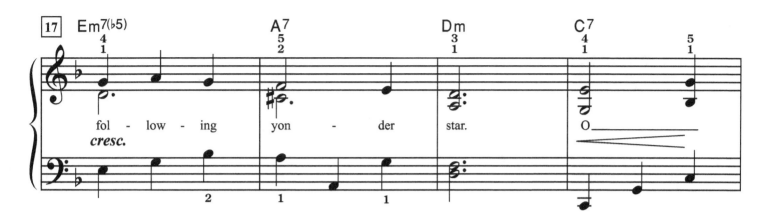

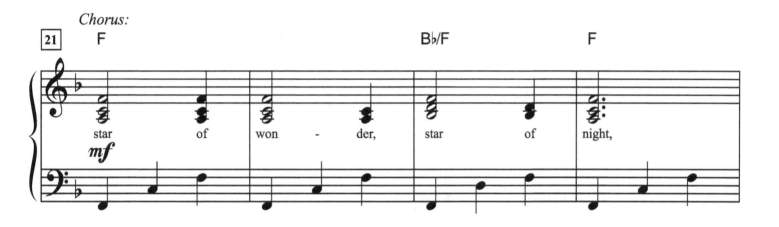

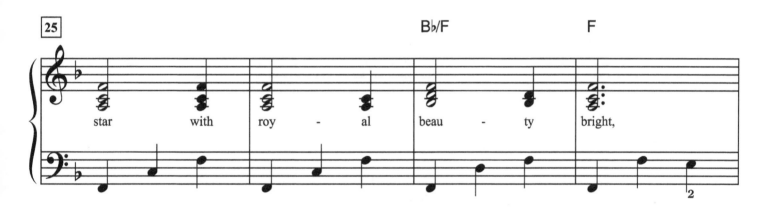

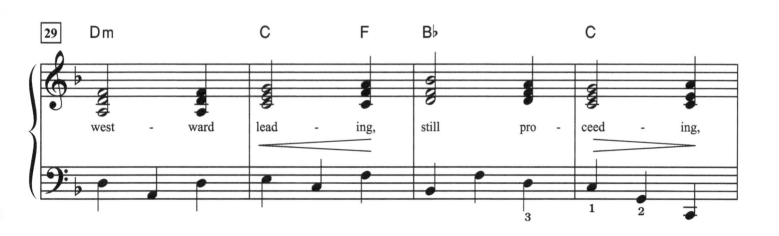

Verse 2:
Born a King on Bethlehem's plain,
Gold I bring, to crown Him again,
King forever, ceasing never
Over us all to reign.
(To Chorus:)

Verse 3:
Frankincense to offer have I,
Incense owns a Deity nigh.
Prayer and praising, all men raising
Worship Him, God most high.
(To Chorus:)

Verse 4:
Myrrh is mine, its bitter perfume
Breathes a life of gathering gloom;
Sorrowing, sighing, bleeding, dying,
Sealed in the stone-cold tomb.
(To Chorus:)

Verse 5:
Glorious now behold Him arise,
King and God and sacrifice.
Alleluia, Alleluia,
Earth to heaven replies.
(To Chorus:)

WINTER WONDERLAND

Words by Dick Smith
Music by Felix Bernard
Arranged by Dan Coates

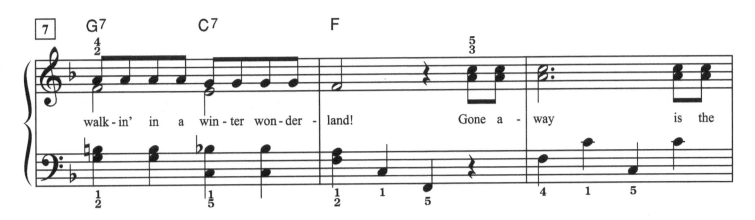

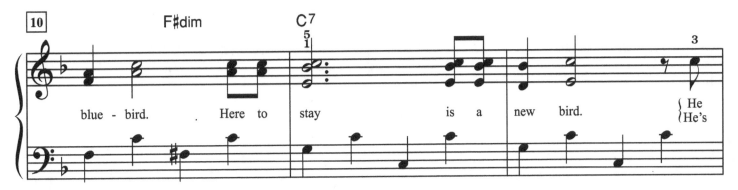

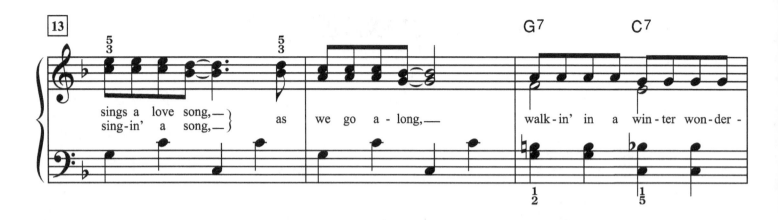

13

sings a love song, —} as we go a-long, — walk-in' in a win-ter won-der-

sing-in' a song, —}

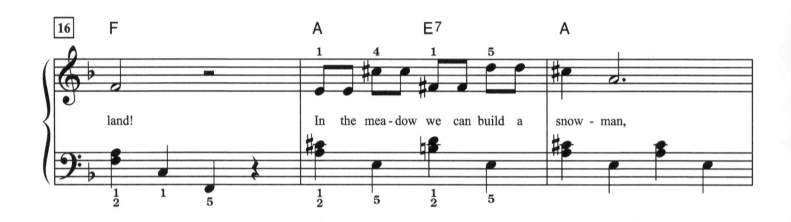

16

land! In the mea-dow we can build a snow-man,

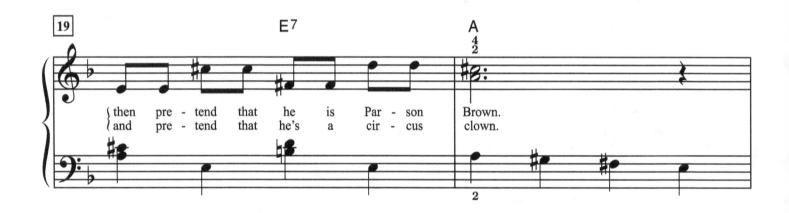

19

then pre - tend that he is Par - son Brown.

and pre - tend that he's a cir - cus clown.

21

He'll say, "Are you mar-ried?" We'll say, "No, man! But

We'll have lots of fun with Mis - ter Snow-man, un -

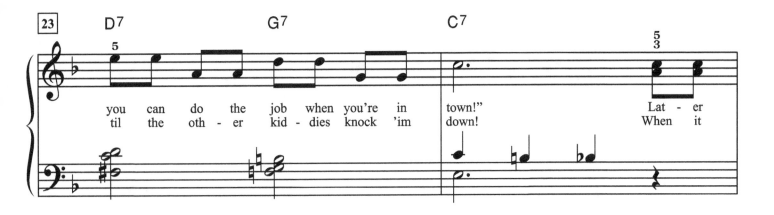

YOU'RE A MEAN ONE, MR. GRINCH

Music by Albert Hague
Lyrics by Dr. Seuss
Arranged by Dan Coates

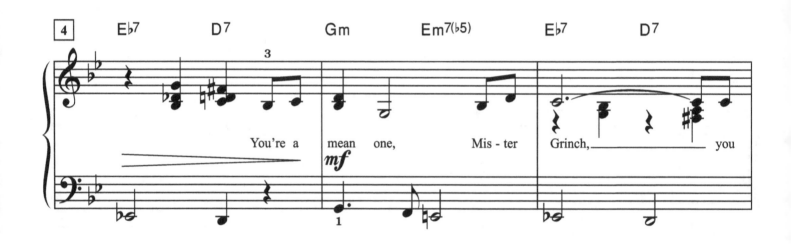

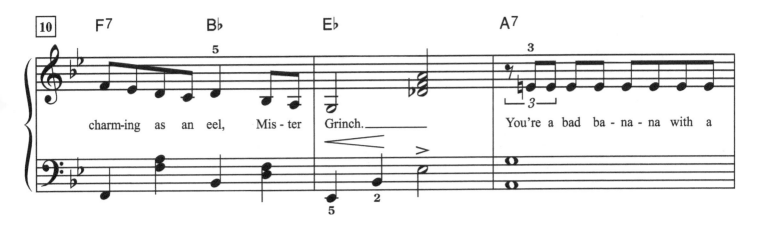

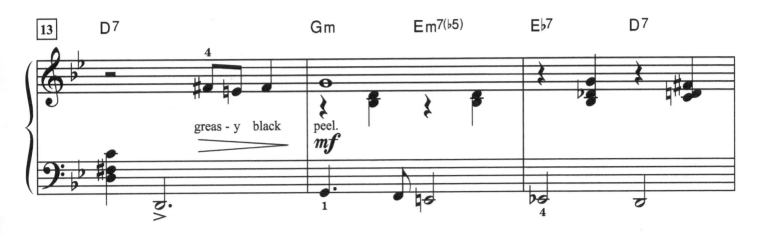

brain is full of spi-ders, you got gar-lic___ in your soul, Mis-ter Grinch.___

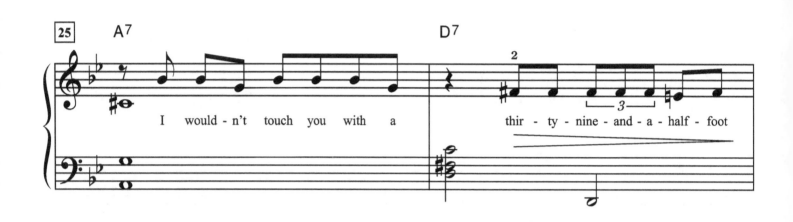

I would-n't touch you with a thir-ty-nine-and-a-half-foot

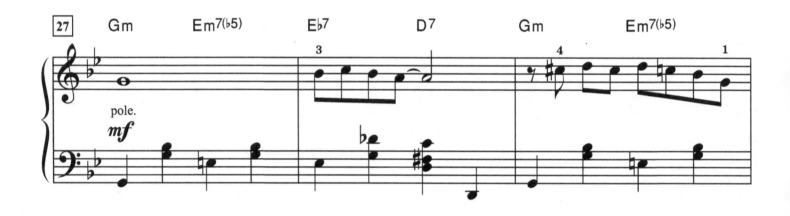

pole.

You're a vile one, Mis-ter Grinch. You have

ter-mites in your smile. You have all the ten-der sweet-ness of a

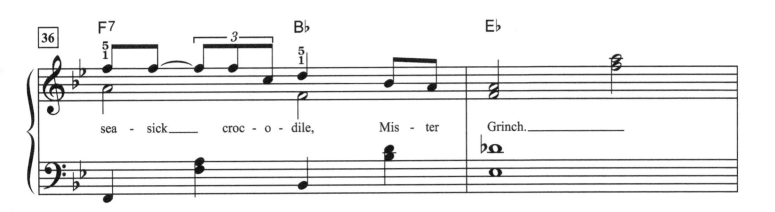

sea - sick___ croc - o - dile, Mis - ter Grinch._____

Giv - en the choice be - tween you, I'd take the sea - sick croc - o -

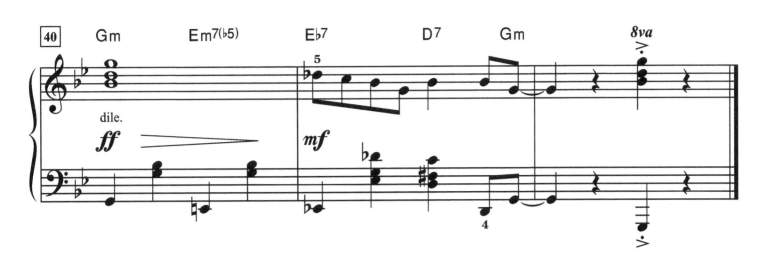

dile.